Praying with
Visionary Women

By Bridget Mary Meehan

SHEED & WARD

Franklin, Wisconsin

As an apostolate of the Priests of the Sacred Heart, a Catholic religious order, the mission of Sheed & Ward is to publish books of contemporary impact and enduring merit in Catholic Christian thought and action. The books published, however, reflect the opinion of their authors and are not meant to represent the official position of the Priests of the Sacred Heart.

1999

Sheed & Ward
7373 South Lovers Lane Road
Franklin, Wisconsin 53132
1-800-266-5564

Printed in the United States of America

Cover and interior art by Doris Klein

Cover and interior design: GrafixStudio, Inc.

Library of Congress Cataloging-in-Publication Data

Meehan, Bridget
    Praying with visionary women / by Bridget Mary Meehan.
       p. cm.
    ISBN 1-58051-063-9 (pbk.)
    1. Catholic women Prayer-books and devotions—English I. Title.
BX2170.W7 M44 1999
242'.643—dc21   99-35188
                                                               CIP

1 2 3 4 5 / 02 01 00 99

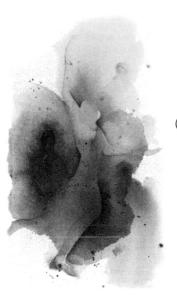

Dedication

To my family
My mother, Bridie Meehan, whose love for family reflected God's tender care and who now rests in God's eternal embrace. My father, Jack, whose warmth and companionship I treasure. My Aunt Molly McCarthy, whose gentle spirit will live forever in my heart. My brothers, Sean and Patrick; my sisters-in-law, Nancy and Valerie; and my niece and nephew, Katie and Danny, who are special blessings in my life.

To all the women whose courage, strength, and wisdom have
reflected to me the love of God as sister and friend
Especially Regina Madonna Oliver, Irene Marshall, Sandra Voelker, Barbara Green, Eileen Dohn, Marcia Tibbitts, Betty Wade, Virginia Fernback, Patricia Byrne, Patricia McAleavy, Kathleen Bulger, Andree Lanser, Peg Bowen, Rea Howarth, Mary Beben, Eileen Melia, Mary Ambrosio, Judy Kalmanek, Peggy Ripp, Cathcrine Kopac, Ginny Koenig, Mary Jean Kane, Kay Graf, Karen Hnat, Nancy Forbes, Estelle Spachman, Stacy Renee, Sharon Friedman, Pam Hoeft, Brenda Adams, Rosemary Walsh, Peggy Gott, Kaye

Brown, Pat Clausen, Jeanne DeSotia, Eileen Thomas, Sharon Danner, Paula Fangman, Kimberly Manthy, Mary Fitzgibbons, Megan Fitzgibbons, Patricia Herlihy, Mary Guertin, Mary Kay Salomone, Kathleen Wiesberg, Donna Mogan, Nancy Healy, Olga Gane, Phyllis Hurst, Evelyn Mulhall, Mary Patricia Mulhall, Kathleen Mulhall, Nancy Mulenex, Eleanora V. Marinaro, Dawn Vehmeier, Consilia Karli, Ellen Coakley, Helen Groff, Gerri Wayne, Luz Sandiego, Roseanne Fedorko, Lynn Johnson, Daisy Sullivan, Michal Morches, Jeanette Kraska, Maria Billick, Doris Mason, Jojo Sandiego, Daisy Sullivan, Andrea Johnson, Ruth Fitzpatrick, Jan Reithmaier, Maureen Fiedler, and the Sisters for Christian Community.

To all the Celtic women in my family
Noreen Davy, Mary D. Meehan, Mary Ferns, Peg Meehan, Margaret Ryan, Mary Tregent, Esther Meehan, Tess Murphy, Elizabeth Murphy, Catherine Murphy, Rose Meehan, Katherine Meehan, Marion Meehan, Kathleen McNamara, Mary Meehan, Alice Meehan, Eileen Meehan and Eileen Preston. To my grandmothers, Bridget Neary Beale and Katie Doyle Meehan, and my Aunt Molly Meehan, whose spirits continue to live within me.

To Mary
Mother and disciple of Jesus, whose companionship reflects sisterly love in the power of Sophia-God.

Special thanks to Doris Klein, for her beautiful art, and to Kass Dotterweich, for her work in editing this manuscript.

To all our foremothers and foresisters in the faith: companions, champions, and change agents in the world.

To all women who live and love as courageous disciples of Jesus in the contemporary world.

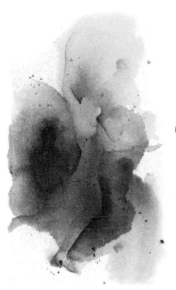

About the Art

The images throughout these pages are an invitation for each of us to dance with the visions we have been given. We, like the women in this book, daily face the challenge of being faithful to the call of the Holy in our own lives. The opportunity to look into the mirrors of their stories is a reminder for us to be authentic in the unfolding of our vision.

Each drawing is intended to translate some of the movement we experience when we, as these women, come face to face with the mystery and challenge of being faithful to the vision. They are offered as another mirror to encourage us to be faithful to the universal task we each have as we discover and unfold the vision implanted within us. The illustrations are intended to reiterate and support the message given by the lives of these visionary women and to be doorways to our story, our struggle, and our summons to BE visionary women and men.

—Doris Klein, CSA

Contents

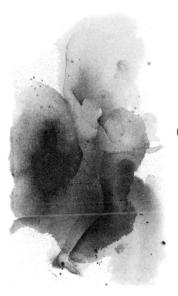

Acknowledgments

I am especially grateful to my family and friends. The gifts of their faith and friendship have touched me deeply. I am especially thankful to my parents, Bridie and Jack Meehan, who taught me so much about God's love by their love for me. I am also grateful to my Aunt Molly McCarthy and her brother Paddy; they were the first members of our family to emigrate from Ireland to the United States in the 1920s. Aunt Molly sponsored our family and provided a home for us in Virginia in 1956.

I am grateful to my brothers and sisters-in-law, Sean and Nancy, Patrick and Valerie, for their support and teasing that keep me grounded in the real world. My niece and nephew, Katie and Danny, have been my mentors, teaching me how to play and delight in the present moment. I am grateful to Irene Marshall for the support she has provided for my family; to Sister Regina Madonna Oliver for her friendship and ideas on this manuscript; for the research that Marsha Tibbits did in preparation of *Praying With Visionary Women;* to Kass Dotterweich for her editorial skills; to Doris Klein for her beautiful artwork which expresses powerful images of the "dance" of visionary women in the circle of life.

Introduction

*I*n 1978 two women on a leave of absence from their traditional religious community to provide care for ailing family members found themselves alone in a spiritual desert without a sign of where they were headed. In prayer they came together as "soul sisters" seeking God's direction. At that time their prayer was simple because they were parched and desperate: "What would you have us do, God? Where are you leading?" The answer came: "You are being led out to a new community with a new vision of shared decision making modeled on the lives of the women in the early Church—women who served their local communities and who experienced Spirit in the nuances of events that occurred in the ordinariness of each day's happenings."

Like Regina and me—in the story above that occurred over twenty years ago—the women who appear on the pages of this book were ordinary women who found God right where they were, in the midst of life's challenges. They were flesh and blood women who knew struggle and pain, who experienced God's love in their innermost beings, and who found the courage to live the gospel. They are women we might have sought out as friends, women many of us would have cherished as soul sisters. Above all, they were women who listened to the Spirit and caught the excitement of a fresher vision that projected creatively beyond their own generation. Fortunately, in the *Kairos* of God's ever presentness, chronological time—even centuries of it—does not separate us from these women. They can be and are as much soul sisters for us as any of our spiritual friends of today.

These are women with whom we can bare our soul, share our feelings, celebrate our successes, mourn our losses, and cherish our visions. Their stories will inspire and touch us as we struggle to live as faithful witnesses to the gospel in our contemporary world. They remind us that abundance is all around us every day, everywhere. They shine light on our path to healing and integration. They challenge us to change unjust structures that oppress and dominate races, cultures, classes, and genders. They call us to tear down the walls that divide, heal the hurts that damage relationships, and build bridges of understanding between spouses, parents, neighbors, strangers, and nations. Like these women, we can become companions, champions, and change agents to everyone we encounter on our spiritual journey. We, too, can become women of vision and prophets to our generation.

Brigit of Kildare: Her spirit lives on today in care-givers of aging and sick parents, and in assertive activists, imaginative visionaries, creative healers, and wondrous celebrators of life, as well as in women and men who are discovering the richness of Celtic spirituality.

Margaret of Scotland: During her reign as Queen of Scotland, Margaret called synods and councils, and initiated a series of ecclesiastical reforms that revitalized the Scottish Church. A generous woman, she shared her time, energy, and material goods with people who were poor and marginalized.

Hildegard of Bingen: All life forms were sacred to Hildegard. Her ecological vision can inspire us to act and live as partners with Earth and with one another for the health and healing of creation. Hildegard preached tirelessly about Church renewal and corresponded with civic and Church leaders.

Clare of Assisi: In a time where men made the rules for women's orders, Clare was the first woman to write her own rule. She championed a simple lifestyle, a message relevant to spiritual seekers today.

Julian of Norwich: Julian proclaimed a nurturing, mothering God to a medieval world too often exposed to a strong-armed, masculine-dominated view of the divine.

Catherine of Siena: As a mystic activist, Catherine joined a women's group associated with the Dominicans rather than being coerced into a cloister. In that way, she was able to serve the poor, minister to the sick, and lecture the pope on what actions he needed to take for the good of the Church.

Joan of Arc: Joan is the patroness of France. She rejected those Church authorities who refused to recognize the validity of her spiritual experiences and call. She is a role model for contemporary women and men who believe in the primacy of conscience and who face condemnation for challenging the abuse of power by autocratic Church leaders.

Teresa of Avila: Teresa was a reformer who renewed the Carmelite order, purifying it of corruption and abuses that had crept in over time. She valued fun and laughter, and provided it among her sisters. She spoke practically and frankly of and to God, and translated her mystical experiences into language ordinary people could understand and relate to. She taught an approach to prayer that can help us experience God's intimate love. We need Teresa's passion for God to be prophets and saints in today's world.

Louise de Marillac: Devoting herself to the poor, Louise made the streets of Paris her convent and ministered tirelessly to the sick and destitute members of society. With Vincent de Paul, her spiritual companion, she brought a new form of religious life into existence in the Church. From her we learn how to dream impossible dreams.

Sor Juana Ines de la Cruz: Sor Juana was a seventeenth-century Latin American feminist who advocated universal education for women. She is a mentor for illiterate women, women scholars, and all women who pursue learning for its own sake. From her we can discover vast treasures of woman-wisdom that can enrich us for generations to come.

Kateri Tekakwitha: Kateri lived simply, truthfully, and courageously. She was faithful to her Native American heritage and to Christ, who came to mean all to her. She reminds us that our gospel commitment requires sacrifice and integrity. She followed the Christian way even when it meant risking everything.

Elizabeth Bayley Seton: A wife, mother, and widow, Elizabeth was a convert to Roman Catholicism at a time when it was not popular to be Catholic. She is the foundress of a religious order dedicated to ministry: the American Sisters of Charity. She displayed a wonderful Christian optimism in the face of tragedy, having buried her husband, her sister-in-law, and several of her children. We can learn much about the life-sustaining power of friendship from reflecting on the love she shared with those around her. On September 14, 1995 she became the first native-born United States saint.

Elizabeth Lange: Elizabeth is the founder of the first religious order of Black women in the United States: the Oblate Sisters of Providence. Her courage can energize us to break racial stereotypes and to be risk-takers in a world where prejudice is still a reality. Like Elizabeth, we need an abundant trust in Divine Providence.

Sojourner Truth: A champion of Black emancipation and women's rights, Sojourner was a former slave. Her journey to freedom has been an inspiration to women and men throughout the world who continue the struggle for civil rights.

Frances Xavier Cabrini: The first United States saint, Frances was an Italian immigrant who established a worldwide missionary institute that ministered to poor, abandoned, and neglected Italian immigrants and their children. From her we learn to care for the abused and afflicted members of our communities.

Therese of Lisieux: Therese is one of the most popular teachers of God's passionate love in our time. In October 1997 she was proclaimed a Doctor of the Church. In her "little way" she explained how ordinary people can live holy lives.

Dorothy Day: As a social activist, Dorothy will be remembered for her radical witness to the gospel among the poor. With Peter Maurin, Dorothy established The Catholic Worker Movement, an organization committed to collaborative decision making and justice advocacy work on behalf of workers.

Catherine de Hueck Doherty: According to Catherine, who fled Russia during the Bolshevik Revolution in 1917, the gospel is the only real revolution the world has experienced. As a powerful witness of gospel living, she practiced what she preached. She tells us that the spiritual journey will bring us poverty, freedom, defenselessness, and "cosmic tenderness" toward all creatures, our sisters and brothers, and ourselves.

Jean Donovan: The profound strength of Jean Donovan and the other Catholic women—Ita Ford, Maura Clarke, and Dorothy Kazel—who were murdered on a deserted road in El Salvador in 1980 reminds us that "no one has greater love than this, to lay down one's life for one's friends."

Thea Bowman: A creative educator, artistic dancer, powerful singer, and dynamic lecturer, Thea may well be remembered as the woman who succeeded in getting the bishops to dance. Thea invites us to preach the gospel with our lives as well as with our words. Like her, we can foster intercultural awareness, understanding, and pride in Black culture and ultimately "go home like a shooting star."

The women in this book are radiant reflections of the feminine face of God. They show us how to be strong witnesses to the Holy One in our midst. These women invite us to experience woman-courage, woman-hope, woman-strength, and woman-passion. Their spirits liberate, energize, and empower us. In prayer, we dialogue with these models of faith. We make them our soul sisters. We establish a relationship with these companions, champions, and change agents who, although with God, are still with us. We argue with these prophetic witnesses to the gospel. We question their decisions and listen to their insights. We share our own stories with them.

These women are our sisters and friends. Their stories touch our souls. Their words are a rich source of inspiration and renewal in our commitment to work for justice, peace, and equality in our world. We can learn much about faith, hope, and love from these daring disciples.

Sisters, daughters, mothers, grandmothers—women of many cultures, races, and ethnic backgrounds—are sharing their dreams and visions to birth a new paradigm of worship, prayer, and community. As the bondage of sexism, racism, militarism, and ageism continues, women prayer groups are exploring a rich variety of resources that celebrate the stories and spirituality of women.

Catch Their Spirit

Praying with Visionary Women invites you to catch the living spirit of amazing women witnesses to the inbreaking of God's wondrous, passionate, infinite love in our midst. In the reflections, discussion starters, and prayer experiences that follow each profile, you are invited to consider each sister in the faith, imaginatively recreate her story from your perspective, and reflect on her words and actions in light of your own life experience.

In the prayer experiences, I recommend that you use a variety of approaches: journaling, poetry, dance, body movement, mime, drama, song, or some artistic form like drawing, painting, sculpting, playing with clay, stamping, or needlepoint. You may wish to use all or some of the prayer suggestions. Listen to your subconscious and try what attracts or excites you. Be conscious of what nourishes your creative spirit—and do it! Trust your lights! They flow from your intuitive inner core where God dwells.

For use as a group, I suggest using one or more of the discussion questions to get people talking about the contributions of these persuasive women and their impact on our hearts and lives. Background music, such as classical or instrumental music, may provide an appropriate setting for reflection and sharing. Before beginning, the group should decide on a facilitator to lead the guided prayer and to organize materials and space for art, journaling, storytelling, body movement, creative activity, and so forth. After everything is ready, the facilitator should read aloud a profile and then invite comments and insights. Members of the group could then share their experiences and/or their responses to the discussion starters. Larger groups might want to break into smaller groups of five or six for the discussion.

Groups can also design creative rituals that celebrate the courageous women's stories that appear in this book. For example, a group might select music for the prayer experiences and movements to accompany the music in which group members can participate. This ritual could begin and/or conclude each session. Singing, humming, dancing, clapping, tapping, moving, swaying to music, and joining hands with others all involve us in body prayer that helps us connect in deep ways.

Group members might want to decide ahead of time to bring symbols of the visionary woman the group will be contemplating. Then, at the conclusion of the prayer experience, the members of the group can share the symbols they brought. After each member shares, she might place the symbol on a special table decorated with cloth, candles, and flowers. The group could then pray a litany or share spontaneous prayers, songs, dance, and/or a group hug. Different members might take turns preparing one of these prayer rituals for each session.

A group might want to consider choosing one or more of the following elements for worship: water, oil, incense, bread, wine, or an art object such as a drawing, painting, or sculpture. The group can then create a simple ritual—such as washing hands, anointing each other with oil, passing the art object around within the group, or breaking and eating bread together—to celebrate the impact that the visionary woman has on people today. Such simple rituals can deepen the group members' relationships with these heroic women and help them become a caring community.

Consider using the human senses —visual, auditory, tactile, and olfactory—in inclusive, communal prayer to open yourself, individually or as a group, to the Spirit's movement. Look at beautiful art, listen to inspiring music, smell perfumed incense, touch soft clay, and/or eat delicious food. This prayer approach invites pray-ers to savor spiritual experiences in rich and often unexpected ways. Recommended Reading (see page 227) offers books that have a variety of ideas for communal rituals.

The wind blows where it wills. Be open to the laughter, tears, insight, and wonder that you may experience—individually and as a group—when you pray with these women of faith and courage. There are no right or wrong ways to pray. Different things work for different individuals and different groups. The important thing is to explore, experiment, share, pray, and celebrate with these daring women role models. Experience the rich legacy of spiritual empowerment that these twenty dynamic, committed women of faith have shared. As you encounter these soul companions, may you dance merrily in God's liberating, loving presence, celebrating the "sacred vision" of your life as a radiant image of the Holy One in our world.

Birthing the Vision

Doris Klein CSA

1.

Brigit of Kildare

Celebrator of Life

Brigit was born around 450. She was the daughter of Dubthach, an Irish chieftain, and Broicsech, a pagan slave woman. Because Brigit lived at the time of transition from pagan to Christian Ireland, the new Church blended her image with that of an older pagan mother goddess of a similar name. With pagan and Christian elements so closely interwoven in the stories of Brigit, it is sometimes difficult to distinguish between the two.

There is a rich collection of legends, myths, tales, and anecdotes that reveal the spirit of Brigit, one of the most acclaimed Irish women ever known. The accounts of Brigit's life from *The Book of Lismore* provide a portrait of a powerful woman wrapped in the mists of myth and legend. Anecdotal testimony from this source describes a life of fantasy and miracle. One such tale tells that, as a tiny infant, Brigit was bathed in milk and thereafter could not eat any food except the milk of a red-eared cow. Brigit is reported to have hung a wet robe on a sunbeam to dry. She healed the sick, caused the mute to speak, turned water into ale, and confronted the devil. Even her clothing possessed healing power.

Brigit is said to have been baptized and named by angels and, according to legend, was the midwife of the Virgin Mary and the godmother to Jesus. She was the protector of poor people and farm animals, and was guardian of the harvest. She increased the yield of cows and sheep and kept the fires burning in the hearths of humble folk.

All this by way of legend.

In reality, Brigit was the most prominent female leader of the Celtic Church. She has become the patron saint of pilgrims and midwives and, like the older Celtic goddess of the same name, she is considered an advocate of women and a patron of learning, art, and poetry.[1]

Brigit of Kildare was revered as a soul sister to the Celtic people for her wisdom, healing powers, and compassionate spirit. Like the female druids of old, her sisters kept a fire burning for hundreds of years as a reminder of Brigit's power to enflame the heart and touch the soul.

As Ireland's first feminist, Brigit was a courageous risk-taker, a faith healer, an ordained bishop, a successful administrator, and an energetic missionary. The following images, stories, and anecdotes reflect a blending of pagan customs with Christian beliefs—a mixture of the pre-Christian mother goddess with the assertive, dynamic, daring, disciple of Christ.

According to an ancient tale, one day Dubthach and Broicsech, Brigit's parents, drove past the house of a druid. When the druid realized it was a chariot, he went out to meet Dubthach and inquired who the woman was in the chariot. Dubthach told him that she was Broicsech, a slave who was pregnant by him. Then the druid prophesied: "Marvelous will be the child that is in her womb. No one on earth will be like her." Dubthach replied sadly, "But my wife wants to sell her." "Never mind," the druid responded, "for the offspring of your wife shall serve the offspring of the slave, for this slave will bring forth a wonderful radiant daughter who will shine like the sun among the stars of heaven."[2]

There are a number of stories about Brigit the healer. One such tale tells of a certain leper who came to Brigit to ask for a cow. Brigit asked him, "Which seems best to you, to take away a cow or to be healed of the leprosy?" The leper said that he preferred to be healed of the leprosy. Brigit prayed and the leper was made whole at once.[3]

Some anecdotes portray Brigit acting like Jesus the healer in the gospels. Once a nun of Brigit's convent became ill and desired milk, but there was no cow near the church at the time. Brigit filled a container with water, blessed it, changed it into milk, and gave it to the nun who recovered immediately.[4]

Other stories remind us of the woman in the gospels who was healed after touching Jesus' garment, and the healing power of Peter's shadow, described in the Acts of the Apostles. Once a poor woman came to Brigit to beg. Brigit gave the woman her own garment and said that it would heal whatever disease or illness to which it was applied. And so it happened, and thus the woman was well from that day forward. On another occasion a certain man from the south of Bregia carried his sick mother on his back, hoping to find Brigit so that she might heal the woman. When the man placed his mother in Brigit's shadow, she was healed.[5]

Brigit dedicated herself to God. *The Life of Brigit* describes her episcopal ordination. Bishop Mel who presided at the ceremony said: "Come, o holy Brigit, that a veil may be placed on your head before the other virgins." Then, filled with the grace of the Holy Spirit, the bishop read the form of ordaining a bishop over Brigit. While she was being consecrated, a brilliant fiery flame ascended from her head. MacCaille, Bishop Mel's assistant, complained that a bishop's rank was bestowed on a woman. Bishop Mel argued: "But I do not have any power in this matter. That dignity has been given by God to Brigit, beyond every other woman. Henceforth, from that time to now the Irish people have given episcopal recognition to Brigit's successor."[6]

This story can provide hope for women who desire ordination. Perhaps the Holy Spirit will "knock our socks off" so to speak — when a bishop gets inspired to ordain a woman priest. Responding to grace, Church leaders sometimes do the most amazing things!

Brigit cherished close relationships with family and friends, and encouraged others to do the same. On one occasion Brigit's foster son, a cleric, was dining with her. After receiving communion, she rang a bell and asked the young man if he had a soul friend. "I have," he answered. "Let us sing his requiem," replied Brigit, "for he has died. I saw when you had eaten half your portion of food that that portion was put in the trunk of your body, but that you were without any head. For your soul friend has died, and anyone without a soul friend is like a body without a head. Eat no more until you get a soul friend."[7]

This story about Brigit reminds us of the need for an "anam cara," a soul friend, a spiritual companion, who helps us discover the treasures hidden within our own souls.

At her dying father's bedside Brigit kept a caring watch while weaving her famous cross of rushes. As companion to her father in his transition from this world to the next, she became an exemplar of a loving daughter whose devotion lasts a lifetime and stretches to eternity's shores. All of us need a soul sister or soul brother who will be there for us in our hour of need. All of us can be like Brigit and share our presence with those who suffer or face loss. The unique "Brigit's cross" worn by many Irish people today bespeaks a culture with a heritage of special care for ill and aging family members, a heritage many modern-day Celts live.

In Kildare Brigit founded a community of women and an adjacent monastery for men, and administered both centers in association with appointed abbots. The Kildare community evolved into a popular center for scholars, saints, artists, and poets. Brigit's convent system grew into a network of institutions in which women could find shelter and refuge from pagan influences, discover ways to be self-sustaining, and obtain an education in their new faith. Some scholars think that Brigit's convents accommodated thousands of women. If this is so, we can certainly imagine that the Kildare community was a place in which women and men used their God-given gifts to make a major contribution to Celtic life and culture.

In the twenty-first century Church, we are witnessing a repeat of history in which mutual relationships and faithful friendships between women and men are pouring new life and vitality into the Church and world. More than likely Brigit would be at home in the many Christian communities today where women and men are proclaiming and living the gospels as disciples and equals.

In a medieval church at Killinaboy, Brigit's image, a *sheela-na-gig* (a figure holding open the entrance to her womb), is carved on the top of the arch to the door, welcoming the community into the church through her "womb." Saint Brigit, like her pre-Christian namesake, was an activist who, mother-like, sought the health, well being, and growth of her "children," the Celtic people.[8] Brigit is a mentor to parents who mourn the rape and murder of their children. She is born again in women and men who act on behalf of justice, peace, and human rights, and who contemplate creation as enveloped in the eternal mystery of God's womb-love. Here all creatures are loved completely. Here all of us belong. Here we celebrate divinity in sun and moon, hills and mountains, rivers and oceans, plants and animals, and in the wondrous mysteries of all things.

Although some historians believe that Brigit never met Patrick, the patron saint of Ireland, the Book of Armagh, an eighth-century manuscript, portrays them as being "of one heart and one mind" and that extraordinary healings occurred in their missionary endeavors. According to one story, "they saw Patrick coming to them. Lassair, an associate of Brigit's, said to her: 'What shall we do for the multitude that has come to us?' Brigit inquired: 'What food have you?' 'There is none,' said Lassair, 'but one sheep, and 12 loaves, and a little milk.' Brigit replied: 'That is good: the preaching of God's word will be made unto us and we shall be satisfied thereby.' After Patrick had concluded the preaching, the food was brought to Brigit that she might distribute it. She blessed it, and the people of God, even Brigit's congregation and Patrick's congregation, were satisfied; and the food left over was more than had been there at first."[9] Here Patrick preached and Brigit presided at Eucharist. Both reflected Jesus who proclaimed the good news and fed the hungry. What an example of partnership in ministry!

The spirit of Brigit of Kildare lives on today, not only in women of Celtic descent, but in all women who focus their energy on the Christian mission. Brigit's compassion for the sick and poor, her ability to heal people and Earth's creatures, her hospitality in inclusive communities, her competency as a wise administrator, her experience of partnership with men in the Church, and her ability to lead as a woman in the Church—all speak to today's women who likewise minister. Brigit's myth lives on in the hearts of women who have a passion for life and who are icons of the many faces of God in our world. Her story connects us to the old religion that predates patriarchy. She bursts upon the scene with a faith that moves mountains and a fiery legacy that ignites the Celtic imagination to this day.

Brigit is an exemplar for women across the globe to be daring activists, imaginative visionaries, creative healers, and wondrous celebrators of life. Let us contemplate the amazing works of Brigit, a spiritual giant, whose life reminds us to be witnesses of grace for this generation.

Reflection

Table Blessing of Brigit

I should like a great lake of finest ale
for the King of Kings.
I should like a table of the choicest food
for the family of heaven.
Let the ale be made from the fruits of faith,
and the food be for giving love.

I should welcome the poor to my feast,
for they are God's children.
I should welcome the sick to my feast,
for they are God's joy.
Let the poor sit with Jesus at the highest place,
and the sick dance with the angels.

God bless the poor,
God bless the sick,
And bless our human race.
God bless our food,
God bless our drink.
All homes, O God, embrace.[10]

Discussion Starters

1. How do the stories, myths, and legends of Brigit of Kildare reflect a woman who is daring? courageous? compassionate? joyous? in tune with her times? a visionary? What images describing Brigit do you find powerful? energizing? healing? exciting? How is Brigit a companion, champion, and change agent in the Celtic Church?

2. What do you think is the significance of the story of the episcopal ordination of Brigit? Have you ever seen Brigit depicted in art, such as on a stained glass window? If so, what symbols—if any—were included in her picture?

3. How do you feel about Brigit's image of heaven as a joyful celebration? What thoughts, feelings, or insights does this image bring to mind?

4. What impact can the story of Brigit have on women today? Was Brigit a feminist? How does Brigit's spirit live on in contemporary women? What contribution does Brigit make to Celtic beliefs, practices, and traditions?

Prayer Experience

(You might want to play lively, instrumental Celtic music during this meditation.)

1. Close your eyes... Relax your body... Breathe deeply and slowly ... Image yourself surrounded by the presence of divine love... Open yourself to God's energy...God's vitality...God's joy... Do something with your body to express your feelings, such as singing, humming, tapping your feet, dancing, or rocking...

2. Reread one of the stories, legends, or myths about Brigit or use her prayer "The Heavenly Banquet." Reread slowly and reflectively...

3. Open yourself to the rich imagery of Brigit... Choose one of the stories from her life... As you reflect on the story, choose one image that moves you... Use this image for in-depth contemplation... Spend as much time as possible with this image... Get in touch with your feelings... If you wish, record your reflections on this experience in a prayer journal or express yourself in poetry, song, dance, art, or in some other creative way...

4. Dialogue with Brigit... Open yourself to this courageous risk-taker...this daring visionary...this enthusiastic missionary...this compassionate healer...this dynamic administrator...this partner in ministry...this woman bishop...this wonderful celebrator of life... Imagine how she can enrich your life...

5. Take time to name your gifts and give thanks for the ways you use them in ministry... Consider how your gifts are similar to and/or different from the gifts of Brigit of Kildare...

6. Be aware of ways that Brigit of Kildare's spirit lives in you...lives in women you know...lives in women of Celtic origin...lives in women from other traditions...other cultures...other races...other nations... Do something to celebrate the inspiring witness of women, like Brigit, in your life.

7. Use the following litany to name and give thanks to God for the times that Brigit of Kildare's spirit has been alive in you. You may want to add your own special prayers of thanksgiving to this litany.

For the times I have discovered fresh energy
for Christian mission in my life
(Pause...Name these times...)
Brigit, thank God with me.

For the times I have shown compassion for the
poor and sick (Pause...Name these times...)
Brigit, thank God with me.

For the times I have been healer to people and
to Earth's creatures (Pause...Name these
times...)
Brigit, thank God with me.

For times when I cared for an aging or sick rel-
ative (Pause...Name these times...)
Brigit, thank God with me.

For the times I have been hospitable and inclu-
sive, opening my heart and world to everyone
(Pause...Name these times...)
Brigit, thank God with me.

For the times I have been partner to men in
ministry (Pause...Name these times...)
Brigit, thank God with me.

For the times I have been visionary, open to
new possibilities and challenging ideas
(Pause...Name these times...)
Brigit, thank God with me.

For the times I have been God's instrument of
amazing miracles, like you, Brigit of Kildare,
(Pause...Name these times...)
Brigit, thank God with me.

Afraid of the Vision

2.

Margaret of Scotland

Champion of Justice

Born in 1046, Margaret of Scotland lived with her family in Hungary as political exiles from the Danish rule of England. Years earlier Margaret's father, a prince of the royal family, had escaped from England and had married a German princess who was related to the Hungarian royal family.

Twelve years later, when it was deemed safe, the family returned to England. Margaret's father died soon after their return, however. When Margaret's life later became endangered as a result of the Norman conquest of England at the Battle of Hastings in 1066, she sought refuge at the court of Malcolm III, King of Scotland. Her admirers described Margaret as beautiful, intelligent, and spiritual. It did not take Malcolm long to fall in love with her and, in 1069, they were married.

The couple's union was happy and a blessing for the Scottish court and nation. Of her eight children, two sons, Alexander and David, became kings of Scotland. Her daughter, Matilda, married Henry I of England, and it is through Margaret and Matilda that the present English royal family can trace their ancestry to the pre-Norman kings of England.[1]

Turgot, who was Prior of Durham and Bishop of Saint Andrews, emphasized Margaret's private and public accomplishments in his biography of her. He described Margaret as a spiritual woman who was devoted to prayer, reading, and almsgiving. Yet the heart of her spirituality is summed up in the following profound words: "that Christ truly dwelt in her heart...what she rejected, he (Malcolm) rejected...what she loved, he (Malcolm), for love of her, loved too!"[2]

Margaret organized prayer, study, and work projects for the members of the court. She began with small changes, such as offering a "grace cup," a special cup of wine for knights who would pray after mealtime. In Scotland the grace cup became known as Saint Margaret's Blessing, and it was used regularly in special Scottish celebrations.

Margaret became a mentor to the women in the royal court. Among her many initiatives, Margaret started a Scripture study group for women.

Along with most women of the day, Margaret loved needlework and, at her request, a room of the castle was set aside for liturgical arts. Here women designed altar cloths, vestments, and other decorations for the liturgy.[3]

Margaret not only visited the poor and sick but also brought into the castle, on a daily basis, some of the neediest people in the area. She would humbly wash their feet before providing them a delicious meal. Although he differed from her in character and personality, Malcolm often followed her example. When he was home, he would join her in this loving act of feet washing. During Advent and Lent, several hundred of the poor were brought into the royal hall and given a sumptuous, courtly repast served by none other than Queen Margaret and King Malcolm.

Throughout her reign, Margaret financially supported over twenty poor people of the kingdom out of the state treasury. When that was depleted, she turned to her husband's personal funds. Fortunately, Malcolm was quite generous with money and resources and supported all of Margaret's charitable ventures, including the almshouses and hospitals that she founded.[4]

For Margaret, an activist, justice was an important part of gospel living. She protested against the abusive behavior of the soldiers toward the people of the countryside and the constant infighting among the Scottish nobles. At Margaret's insistence, Malcolm initiated efforts to stop the violence and bickering. Ever the vigilant overseer, she sent her own agents to determine if the Scots were abusing their Anglo-Saxon captives. If this proved to be the case, Margaret would pay the ransom money and release the English prisoners. Though Margaret was vehemently opposed to the inhumanity of warfare, Malcolm felt his ongoing battle with England necessary for Scottish independence. Nonetheless Margaret fasted for long periods of time for the end to the brutal conflict.[5]

During her reign, Margaret initiated a series of ecclesiastical reforms that revitalized the Scottish Church. Religious issues and Church policies were among her major concerns. Certain liturgical practices and abuses that had crept in at that time had weakened the faith of the community. Disturbed by the complacent attitude of the clergy and hierarchy, Margaret called synods and councils to listen to Church officials, to express her perspectives on religious matters, to confront corruption, to foster intellectual development, and to promote Christian living.[6]

Clearly Margaret was a change agent who took responsibility for effecting the transformation of the Church. As a herald of gospel values to the Church and state, she not only did charitable works but also made justice her goal. A wise and discerning woman, Margaret knew what to do and used her political influence as queen to bring about the changes that would benefit the people of Scotland.

In these synods and councils, Margaret did not assume the role of passive facilitator. Rather she took a proactive role and was clearly in charge. She had definite opinions about the issues at hand and was forthright in expressing her reform agenda. She advocated the practice of Easter communion and abstinence from manual labor on Sundays. She also played an important role in establishing monasteries, churches, and hostels for pilgrims. She supported the revival of Iona Abbey and founded Holy Trinity Abbey at Dunfermline, which would become the Scottish Westminster Abbey and serve as a burial place for its royal family. In the arenas of politics and religion, Margaret brought a powerful English influence to Celtic Scotland. In

1673 she was named patron saint of Scotland and is the only Scottish saint in the Roman calendar. Her feast is celebrated on November 16.[7]

Margaret was a prominent woman of her times. Her words and deeds proclaimed the Good News of the gospel to the people of Scotland. She warned against the kind of blindness that turned the dark into light and evil into good. Truth, not success, was important to her. As a companion to the king and a champion for the poor, Margaret was an activist who used her influence to promote a peace-making and justice agenda for Church and society. She challenged the Church to change and encouraged adequate preparation for the clergy. Her achievements included liturgical and spiritual renewal that revitalized the Christian faith of the people. She was a leader that led by doing—by serving the poor and working for justice. A woman with a vision, Margaret continues to inspire us to work for systemic change in our world.

Today the poor are waiting, the oppressed are struggling, the Church is changing. Will we see the suffering Christ in their faces? We have the responsibility to try. We can be people of prayer and activism who take risks for peace, justice, and reform. Like Margaret, and others before us who have taken risks for gospel values, we need to hear and respond to the word of God calling us through the needs of people around us. We can bind up the wounds of people and challenge the systems that cause their suffering. Like Margaret, who did what she could when it was needed, we can offer spiritual leadership in our century that will give hope to many. Perhaps it will change everything.

Reflection

[During the reign of Queen Margaret] the Church of Scotland comes in for scrutiny too. It disturbs her that liturgical practices have crept in which differ from the rest of the Western Church, for she understands the tremendous unifying strength of a universal liturgy with the symbolic value of uniformity from one end of Europe to the other. As to people failing to receive the Eucharist, holding the sacrament in such awe that they feel too unworthy, she exclaims: "What! Shall no one that is a sinner taste that holy mystery? If so, then it follows that no one at all should receive it for no one is pure from sin." Citing the Gospel as well as commentaries by Church Fathers to convince the faithful of the graces available, she induces many to return to a reception of the Eucharist not only at Easter but on other feasts too.[8]

Discussion Starters

1. Margaret of Scotland was a companion and mentor to Malcolm in their ministry to the poor. In what ways have you witnessed civil leaders in ministry to the poor in your area? nation? world? How and with whom do contemporary leaders work for systemic justice and change in our world?

2. Margaret was a champion for justice for the poor and oppressed members of society. Who are the poor and oppressed in our society? What are their needs? How are you called to be a champion for justice in your area?

3. As an activist and reformer, Margaret was a change agent. She protested violence in society and abuse in the Church. She worked with others to bring about change in both institutions. How are modern women called to be change agents in society and Church?

4. Margaret took a position on liturgy and reception of Eucharist. Do you agree or disagree with her view? Why? What are the great issues around Eucharist in our time? What position do you hold on them?

Prayer Experience

1. Breathe slowly and consciously… Let go of any outer or inner distractions… When you become aware of any thoughts, desires, or feelings, simply let them go… As you breathe in and out, use one of the following prayer words to help you center: "Jesus," "Shaddai," "God," "Sophia," "Shekinah," or a prayer word of your choice…

2. Reflect on Margaret of Scotland's perspective on the Eucharist… Reflect on the meaning of Eucharist in your life… Think of yourself as the yeast in the bread sent to nourish the poor, sick, and homeless… See yourself as a loaf of bread given for hungry refugees… Image yourself as the bread at Eucharist that must be broken so that Jesus may be food for those in the assembly… Imagine yourself nourishing someone today with kindness…with generosity…with compassion…with justice…with truth…with courage…with strength… with faith…with hope…with love… Realize that you are the bread of life… Give yourself as the body of Christ to the Body of Christ…

3. Reflect on Margaret of Scotland as a companion with her husband in ministry… Reflect on Margaret as a champion of justice for the poor, sick, needy, and oppressed members of society… Reflect on Margaret as a protester against violence and ecclesiastical abuse… Image Margaret as a reformer…as an activist…as a change agent in Church and society… Be aware of any hopes or dreams her gospel living inspires in you… Write a letter to Margaret expressing your thoughts, feelings, hopes, and dreams.

4. Reflect on ways you have experienced companionship with others in ministry… Reflect on how you have been a champion for the poor, sick, needy, and oppressed members of society… Reflect on ways you have protested against violence and ecclesiastical abuse…

Reflect on ways you have worked for reform in Church and society in the past... Offer thanks for these graced opportunities...

5. Be aware of the core gospel values of your life... Reflect on any issues of justice that these values stir within you... Now image yourself as an activist working with others to bring about systemic change in Church and society... Be aware of any thoughts, feelings, images, or sensations that emerge...

6. Visualize the infinite love of the Holy One flowing through you as you passionately work for justice for the oppressed in Church and society... Image a different Church and society where justice prevails...where peace prevails...where equality prevails...where love prevails...

7. Draw an image or symbol of this new world or Church where justice, peace, and equality prevail. Hang it in a prominent place as a reminder of your hope for the future.

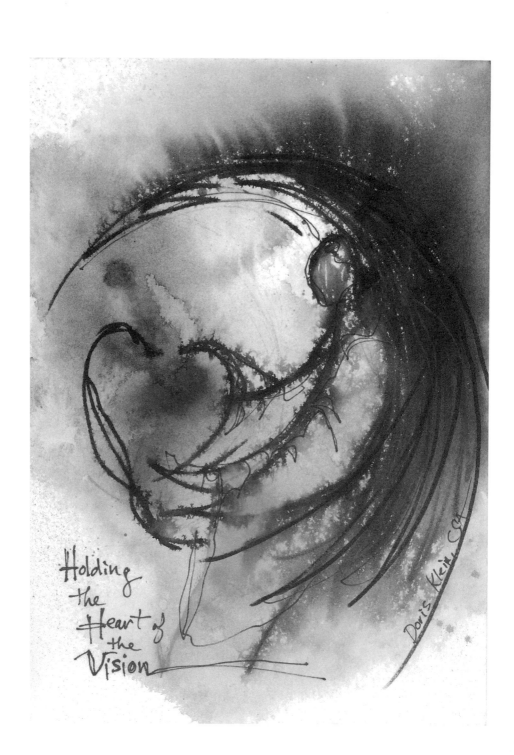

Holding
the
Heart of
the
Vision

Doris Klein CSA

3.

ℋildegard of Bingen

Preacher of Renewal, Friend of Earth

ildegard of Bingen was born in 1098, the tenth child of an upper-class family in Bickelheim, Germany. At the age of eight, Hildegard was placed under the care of Jutta, an anchoress who educated her in the Benedictine tradition. At eighteen she joined the Benedictine community and in 1136, after Jutta's death, Hildegard became abbess of the twelve-member community at Disibodenberg.

At the age of forty-two Hildegard experienced mystical visions that transformed her life. A brilliant light came from heaven, she recalled, which "kindled my whole heart and breast like a flame, not burning but warming, as the sun warms anything on which its rays fall. And suddenly I grasped the underlying meanings of the books— of the Psalter, the Gospels and other Catholic books of the Old and the New Testament."[1]

Hildegard immediately became ill, and it was not until she started to write about these visions that she recovered. She spent the next ten years writing *Scivias,* which means "Know the Ways," to share her experience of illumination that helped her accept God's call for her life.

Hildegard's reputation as a visionary holy woman spread throughout Europe. Leaders from civil and Church life sought her advice: Thomas Becket, Fredrick Barbarosa, and Bernard of Clairvaux. Like the prophets of old, she preached an unpopular message of reform to Church officials.

Tirelessly Hildegard embarked on four preaching tours, attacking the corruption and abuses of the Church. In crowded cathedrals all over Germany she proclaimed the good news of salvation to the people of God and admonished clerics for failing to teach and live the Christian life. Reproving Pope Anastasius 1V, she wrote: "Wherefore, O man, you who sit on the papal throne, you despise God when you embrace evil. For in failing to speak out against the evil of those in your company, you are certainly not rejecting evil. Rather you are kissing it. And so the whole world is being led astray through unstable error, simply because people love that which God cast down."[2]

Hildegard not only preached justice and integrity, but she lived it. She believed the law of God took precedence over the laws of the Church. On one occasion Hildegard made a difficult decision that set her at odds with the local archbishop. Apparently a man who had been excommunicated by the Church was buried in the monastery cemetery. Several days after his interment, Church officials ordered his body exhumed and threatened Hildegard's community with interdict—which meant her nuns could not receive the sacraments or sing the divine office—if it did not comply. In response, Hildegard defended the dead man's spiritual status, informing her superiors that he had repented and received the sacraments before he died. When this did not work, she made sure that no inscriptions were left that would identify his grave. After consultation with her sisters, a decision was made: Hildegard chose interdict. She wrote about how she arrived at this conscience decision: "I looked, as is my wont, to the true light and saw in my soul with open eyes that if, according to their instruction, the body of this dead man be cast out, that act would threaten great danger to our place, like a great darkness, and the blackness of a cloud which presages storm and thunder would ever cloud us."[3]

Admonishing the archbishop for his harsh punishment of her community, Hildegard warned that those who silence the music of liturgical worship will be condemned in eternal life "without the company of the angelic songs of praises in heaven." Soon after, the interdict was removed and the following year Hildegard died—on September 17, 1179.[4]

Hildegard believed that women and men are equal partners in doing God's work. She taught that women were called to be prophets in the male-dominated society of her era, because the male clergy had become weak and lukewarm in living their God-given call. Scholar Bernhard W. Scholz comments on Hildegard's prophetic impact: "She claimed that now woman rather than man—obviously Hildegard herself—was to do God's work. It is difficult not to see in her visionary experience and activism, as well as her claim for the mission of woman in a male-dominated age, a gesture of protest, the reaction of an intelligent and energetic woman who chafed under the restraints imposed on women by the culture in which she lived."[5]

Pope John Paul II affirmed Hildegard's greatness as a mentor for our age. In 1979, on the eight-hundredth anniversary of her death, the pope called Hildegard "an outstanding saint," a "light to her people and her time [who] shines out more brightly today."[6]

Hildegard's ideas and imagery are more popular today than ever before, perhaps because she saw the interconnection of all created beings. She rejoiced in the beauty of water, land, sky, and life. The Earth, as Hildegard envisioned, is our common home and the dwelling place of divinity among us.

Contemporary seekers can find food for reflection in Hildegard's writings, which glimpse the natural world aglow with God. Her words challenge our anthropocentrism and help us discover our place in the natural world. God is in all things. When we touch a tree in our backyard or pick up a tiny rock in our neighborhood creek, we embrace the body of God. Every created thing reflects the glory of God. God's love flows through all things and is manifested everywhere in our world. Hildegard's words remind us to massage the Earth with our feet as we walk on holy ground every day of our lives: "I am the breeze that nurtures all things green. I encourage blossoms to flourish with ripening fruits. I am the rain coming from the dew that causes the grasses to laugh with the joy of life."[7]

As we enter the new millenium, we need the spirit of our soul sister, Hildegard, to guide us as we strive to honor Earth as a beloved friend. Like Hildegard, we can be mystics who make connections that nurture life and proclaim the holiness of our fellow creatures. We can commit ourselves to preserving a healthy environment for the natural world. We can live simply, peacefully, justly, and joyfully as we touch the Earth with gentleness and share our resources with needy people around the globe.

Like Hildegard, we can be prophets as we commit ourselves to do justice for Earth and for the Church. We can expand women's roles, listen to women's wisdom, and involve women in policy making in all our institutions. We can speak the truth in love to everyone. From the Middle Ages, Hildegard awakens us to a powerful vision of God present in creation. As we enter the twenty-first century, we can continue her exploration into the depths of God's glory that can be found everywhere on Earth and in the heavens. All we need are eyes to see and ears to hear.

Reflection

O Holy Spirit, you make life alive, you move
in all things, you are the root of all created
being, you waken and reawaken everything
that is.[8]

O mighty passage, penetrating all
in the heights, upon the earth,
and in all deeps,
you bind them and gather them all together.

From you the clouds have their flowing,
the ether its flight,
the stones their moisture,
the waters spurt forth in streams,
and the earth exudes verdure.[9]

Discussion Starters

1. How can we awaken to the Spirit dwelling in our lives and in our world? Are we called to be mystics today? If so, how can we respond to this call?

2. How are we, like Hildegard, called to be prophets today? What challenges will we face if we choose to speak the truth to power in Church and society?

3. What is our place in the natural world? How can we befriend Earth?

4. What can you do to promote ecological balance and environmental responsibility? How can you celebrate the sacredness of Earth in your worship and prayer?

Prayer Experience

1. The Hebrew word for Spirit is Ruach, which means breath. God breathes in us—we are alive. Become aware of your breath... Each time you breathe, realize that Spirit is moving in you... enlivening you... awakening you to life... Focus your awareness on your breathing...breathing in and out slowly... Your breathing is your prayer...

2. As you continue breathing deeply and slowly, be conscious of Spirit living in you...dwelling in your body...dwelling in your mind...dwelling in your spirit... Open yourself to images, visions, or dreams that Spirit has for you...

3. Pray one of these mantras: "God's Spirit embraces me" or "I am Spirit's dwelling place"... Consider creating your own affirmation of

God's Spirit moving in you... As you repeat your prayer, awaken more deeply to the love...to the strength...to the power...to the goodness...to the courage...to the compassion...of God within you... (Repeat for several minutes or as long as you desire.)

4. Pray one of these mantras: "God's Spirit flows through me to __ (name person(s)__" or "I bring Spirit's peace, justice, compassion, truth, and kindness to __ (name person(s)__." As you repeat your prayer, image God's Spirit touching, healing, liberating, and transforming the people you are praying for...

5. Bring your hands near your mouth and blow your breath into your hands as a prayer of thanksgiving for food, drink, and your favorite blessings... (As each blessing comes to mind, blow into your hands.)

6. Slowly raise your arms above your head and image Spirit speaking to you through nature... Offer thanks to sun, moon, stars, wind, clouds, rain, and creatures of Earth for their presence...

7. Take your shoes off, touch the Earth gently, and massage the ground with your feet to express your connection with the natural world... Conclude your prayer by kissing Earth, caressing a plant, singing with a bird, dancing with the wind, or celebrating your communion with creation in whatever way you feel most comfortable.

Pleading for
Vision

4.

Clare of Assisi

Witness to Simplicity

C lare was born to Favarone and Ortulana Offreduccio in 1194 in Assisi, Italy. Her parents were of the noble wealthy and lived in a large house on the Piazza of San Rufino. According to legend Clare's mother, Ortulana, received a vision that her child would be a magnificent light of God's presence in the world.

As a young woman Clare demonstrated a passionate love for Jesus that attracted other women. Her relatives and neighbors, Pacifica, Cristiana, and Filippa, shared prayer and a communal life with Clare in her home. They became soul friends for one another, models of sanctity and mutual support. Clare also made a private vow of virginity and sold her property as a clear indication that she did not want to marry into nobility. In doing this, Clare challenged societal expectations that women were dependent on men for their identity and status. Clare charted a new path for women by living the gospel according to her inner wisdom. She blazed a trail that women throughout the centuries would follow.

Scholars believe that Francis of Assisi probably visited Clare in her home before 1212, when he was in the process of founding his order. He was inspired by Clare's reputation for holiness. Ingrid J.

Peterson, author of *Clare of Assisi: A Biographical Study,* believes that Clare, a strong self-directed woman, may have been a spiritual mentor who helped the itinerant preacher realize his own dream of transformation in Christ. "Seeing the wholeness in Clare, Francis may have been helped to realize the possibilities for his own conversion. Likewise, Clare's originality lay in her unique response to the images within herself and others. Her creativity was in her response to her inner truth."[1]

More than likely Clare was the kind of soul sister Francis needed to nurture his spiritual vision of living the gospel simply, freely, and joyfully. Clare and Francis were close friends who gave each other mutual support and strength. They shared a dream that would help renew the Church.

On Palm Sunday, according to the local custom, young women from the upper class would dress in their loveliest apparel and process up to the bishop to receive their palm branches. "On this particular Palm Sunday (1212) Clare's turn came to go forward, but she did not rise.... Perhaps she slipped into a kind of rapture. It is public record, in any event, that the bishop saw her sitting with her family immobile, and walked down to hand her the palm himself." Her biographers believe that this experience was a defining moment in her life.[2]

That evening Clare opened a door that had been secured with an iron bar and quietly slipped out of her home. Accompanied by a friend, she walked to Saint Mary's Church in Portiuncula, where Francis and his brothers greeted her, tonsured her hair, and gave her a tunic to wear. Then Clare sought refuge from her family at the Benedictine monastery of San Paolo de Abbadesse, which had been designated as an official sanctuary for anyone who lived there. Although violators could incur excommunication, Clare's family pursued her there nonetheless. *The Legend of St. Clare* describes her dramatic resistance to her male relatives: "They employed violent force, poisonous advice, and flattering promises, trying to persuade her to give up such a worthless deed that was unbecoming to her class and without precedent in her family. But taking hold of the altar cloths, she bared her tonsured head, maintaining that she would in no way be torn from the service of Christ."[3] After Frances and his brothers renovated San Damiano, Clare and her sister, Catherine, took up residence there, and were soon joined by other women. Clare called the group the Poor Ladies, now known as the Poor Clares.

At the age of fifty-five, Clare was the first woman to write a rule for religious life. Her precepts exhibited a free spirit and a common-sense approach to community living. The strict laws of enclosure and fasting were flexible and adaptable to the circumstances of the sisters' lives; exceptions were allowed. Clare's approach maintained a balance between prayer and work. Unlike the rule written by Pope Innocent IV for the Poor Ladies, which reflected a male, hierarchical approach, Clare's rule offered a more feminine, relational model of community. The contrast between Pope Innocent's rule and Clare's rule is evident. As Carol Flinders observes: "He makes the sisters sound like prisoners one minute and wanton temptresses the next.... He seems obsessed with maintaining a strong line of authority. Clare's, in contrast, emanates joy and gratitude for the vocation itself and deep respect for those who shared it with her."[4] On August 9, 1253, two days before she died, Clare's rule received papal approval. Two years after her death, on August 12, 1255, Clare was canonized.

Clare was a woman who knew that God spoke through women. Determined to follow her vision of religious life in spite of opposition, she let nothing and no one dissuade her from passionate gospel living. A model for women under pressure to live up to others' expectations, Clare challenges us to live by our own deep truth and to be guided by our own inner wisdom, so that God's truth shines forth in all our choices. God speaks, God lives, and God rejoices in women everywhere, like Clare.

Independent women in the twenty-first century who are trying to define their identity in a male-dominated society and Church can find inspiration in Clare, who chartered a new course for women in religious life. She would understand the challenge women face today in living as equals with men. In the end, Clare succeeded. So, too, will today's women. Clare teaches them to listen to their inner wisdom, the voice of truth in their own souls. She inspires them to let the old structures that foster patriarchy fall away and to pioneer new structures that promote equality and justice. Although women and men are building mutual relationships in the home, workplace, and Church, some of us may have to wait for this vision to become a full reality. But we can be assured that it will evolve in God's time!

Clare understood that love and poverty are connected. She taught that poverty frees one from the bondage of material things and from all the things that clutter the human heart and soul. This liberation is necessary in order to love one's neighbor. For Clare, poverty opens the heart to receive the gift of God in the depths of the soul. She believed that following Jesus in this way reveals the powerful presence of the Holy One in our lives in an unsurprising way. Clare's words continue to inspire us to live the gospel wholeheartedly:

> What you hold, may you [always] hold.
> What you do, may you [always] do and never
> abandon.
> But with swift pace [and] light step
> and feet unstumbling,
> so that even your steps stir up no dust,
> go forward
> securely, joyfully and swiftly
> on the path of prudent happiness.[5]

Gospel poverty was at the heart of Clare's rule. The Poor Ladies owned nothing; they lived simply without property, endowments, or any kind of material possessions. For Clare, doing without things led to deep communion with God. Her way of life was characterized by a deep trust in God to provide for the needs of the community. Whatever the Poor Ladies received was sufficient. Openness and receptivity reflected Clare's attitudes toward people and things. For her, everything was gift. She and her "ladies" lived the gospel passionately according to the Franciscan ideal.

Through the centuries Clare has continued to be a beacon of light to women and men who long to love Christ with an undivided heart, to serve others generously, and to live simply in a world that glorifies material possessions. If we have too many clothes in our closets, too much money in the bank, too many things cluttering our lives, Clare can help us find the one thing necessary—God who will liberate and fill our emptiness with divine love. Our conversion process may take time—sometimes years—but we will experience freedom and joy when we live with a loose grasp on material things, when we are willing to share our possessions as well as our time and energy with those in need. Then we will experience what Clare and her Poor Ladies experienced in the thirteenth century—that God will not be outdone in generosity. Abundance will be ours, too, pressed down and overflowing.

Like the Poor Ladies, we can open our hearts and hands to receive God's gifts that are right in front of us every day. The Precious Presence is all around us. How often do we take a deep breath and appreciate—really appreciate—the air we breathe? How often do we savor the food we taste and smell the flowers along our path? When was the last time we listened to our child, laughed with a friend, embraced our spouse? It is true that the best things in life are free, but we are often too distracted or too busy to see the simple treasures of life right in front of us. Clare teaches us that prayer will bring us the balance we need and that God will show us the path to serenity.

When we feel stressed by too much activity and not enough time to rest, we can simply take a deep breath to calm our body and smile as we contemplate the wonders of life all around us. Like Clare, we need prayer to illuminate the presence of God that dwells within us and within all things. Each of us bears God's thumbprint. Each of us is created as a unique expression of divine love in the world. As we still our souls, we will discover God's presence everywhere. In everyone we meet, we will see the face of God. We simply need eyes to see, ears to hear, and a heart to love the holy in our midst. If we live the gospel radically, like Clare, our life will be like hers—a sacred adventure.

Reflection

In a letter to Agnes of Prague, Clare expressed the mutual love and support that was at the heart of the Poor Ladies' life:

> I beg you to receive my words with kindness and devotion, seeing in them at least the motherly affection that in the fire of charity I daily feel toward you and your daughters to whom I warmly commend myself and my daughters in Christ.[6]

Discussion Starters

1. What message do you think Clare of Assisi brings to contemporary society?

2. What impact do female models of sanctity, like Clare and her Poor Ladies, have on women and men in a materialistic world?

3. Clare and Francis shared a close personal relationship and a mutual commitment to the same vision of the gospel. What can women and men learn from their partnership in the gospel?

4. Clare expressed a deep affection for her sisters. How can women benefit from joining together in mutual support to share their spiritual journeys?

Prayer Experience

1. Take a few deep breaths... Slowly inhale through your nose... Slowly exhale through your mouth... Inhale... Exhale... Close your eyes and invite your body to relax... Begin at your forehead and relax each muscle group, moving down your body to the soles of your feet... As each part of your body relaxes, let go of all tension and discomfort... If there is any area of your body that is not completely relaxed, simply breathe deeply and send relaxation to that area...

2. Journey to the depths of your soul... Be still there in the presence of Love Divine... Be aware that your ultimate authority is the divine voice within your own soul...

3. Get in touch with your deepest self, your inner wisdom... Notice what you see...what you hear...what you feel... Ask Sophia, the Wisdom of the Ages, to reveal to you new thoughts...creative ideas...daring dreams... Open yourself to God's vision for your life...

4. Imagine Clare of Assisi joining you and some of your favorite friends for a spiritual dialogue... Visualize Clare's tremendous energy and power touching you...connecting you with her woman-wisdom...with her woman-passion...with her woman-courage... Listen as Clare shares the mutual love and support that was at the heart of the Poor Ladies' life... Imagine what this could mean for your understanding of friendship with women...with men... Share with Clare your gratitude for the love and support of your friends... Offer a prayer of thanksgiving for your close friendships...

5. Image Clare giving you a letter containing a special message for you... Reflect on its meaning in your life... Hear Clare offer you the affirmations and advice you need to hear... Decide on how you will process or respond to this message...

6. Breathing deeply, let go of any stress you may be feeling from having too much to do and too little time… Let go of any stress you may be feeling from relationship problems…from job worries…from financial concerns…from physical conditions… Visualize yourself placing these stresses in a balloon and watching the balloon float upward into the sky…until you cannot see it anymore… Be aware of how you feel as you let go of the balloon carrying all your worries… Imagine how you might be able to live a more balanced life… Imagine yourself acting as if you were living this way… Imagine how your life would be different… Imagine how you would feel…how you would act… Let this balance and harmony flow into you and out of you as you relax deeply into the acceptance and love of divine wisdom dwelling in your innermost center… See yourself celebrating life as a sacred adventure…

7. Imagine yourself living more simply with less things…with more time…with more energy… Imagine the things you would get rid of…the clutter you would remove… Imagine how you would spend your time…your energy…your money… See yourself celebrating the simple abundance of life… Dance, sing, jump for joy, paint a picture, compose a poem, or draw an image—or simply be in love with God and with all creation.

If you belong to a women's group, plan a festive celebration in honor of your choice to live more freely, joyfully, and abundantly.

Consumed
by the
Vision

5.

Julian of Norwich

Proclaimer of the
Feminine Face of God

One of the most popular soul sisters of our times is the fourteenth-century English anchoress and great spiritual writer, Julian of Norwich. Born in 1342, Julian lived an independent life of solitary prayer in a small room attached to Saint Julian's Church. Little is known about her early life. Although she refers to herself as "unlettered," the literary skills she demonstrates in her writings make it apparent that Julian was a woman of learning. Some historians think she was educated by the Benedictines at Carrow.

A wise and caring woman, Julian offered words of healing and comfort to those who sought her spiritual advice. Her witness to God's love in an era of societal turmoil and change transcends time and continues to speak powerfully to contemporary seekers.

Julian lived in the era of the black death, peasant revolts, and the Great Schism. It was a time when military leaders, nobles, and kings exploited the efforts of poor workers, whose attempts at uprising were futile. While the bubonic plague killed thousands throughout Europe, scandal, division, and crisis pervaded the Church, with three claimants to the papacy, each excommunicating the other. In this dark era, when people needed something to help them endure the suffering and injustice around them, a God-centered woman named Julian came on the scene with a message of faith, hope, and love. She inspired confidence in spiritual seekers that no matter what happened, God's presence is near and "all manner of things will be well."

Julian knew this because God had told her. At the age of thirty, during an illness, Julian received sixteen visions, which she called "Showings." In these encounters with Christ Julian glimpsed divine love transforming all of life. Her visions reveal a deep understanding of the indwelling presence of a loving God in the depths of our souls. According to Julian's perceptions, we are all abundantly blessed by a God who loves us and who reveals the divine self to us through life's journey. We can savor the goodness of God, which surrounds us always and is able to satisfy the deepest desires of our hearts: "It seems to me that when the Holy Spirit touches the soul it longs for God rather like this, 'God, of your goodness give me yourself, for you are sufficient for me…. If I were to ask less, I should always be in want. In you alone do I have all.'"[1]

It is clear that the boundless love of God was a passionate, powerful experience that energized Julian's whole being and influenced her view of life. She understood the Trinity as a divine intimate relationship of the "Maker, Keeper, and Lover," who envelops us in the storms and difficulties of life with an enduring love that "clothes us, enfolds us and embraces us; that tender love completely surrounds us, never to leave us."[2]

In her mystical encounters with the Holy One, Julian discovered the feminine face of God and Christ. She shared that discovery with us in female imagery that challenges us to raise the God question in every age. Julian's words provide a powerful revelation of God's feminine face echoed in Scripture and Christian tradition through the ages: "As truly as God is our Father, so truly is God our mother. To the property of motherhood belong nature, love, wisdom and knowledge, and this is God… We have our being from him (Jesus Christ) where the foundation of motherhood begins with all sweet protection of love which endlessly follows…the mother can give her child a suck of milk, but our precious Mother Jesus can feed us with himself and does."[3]

Since God is transcendent—beyond all names—no image can describe the divine mystery. God is so much more than we have ever imagined or known. Thus to use exclusive masculine concepts with reference to God is to stifle the development of women and men in the Church. Julian, wise theologian that she was, knew this and provided us with a new understanding of God's feminine presence.

Contemporary women and men are experimenting with God language that refers to God as "Mother" as well as "Father." As we liberate God from exclusive masculine language, women and men are coming to a deeper realization of themselves as created in God's image. Many contemporary theologians affirm the use of feminine God metaphors to enrich the prayer and worship of the Church.

Using feminine imagery to balance our understanding of God liberates the Church from patriarchy's domination. It provides contemporary women and girls the gender identification with God that men and boys have always had. When women and men can pray comfortably with both masculine and feminine images of God, they will relate to God with a fuller sense of who God is—and who they are. No longer will our Church worship an inadequate God.

Julian's message is as important today as it was in medieval England. In an age where paradigms are shifting, shaking up institutions, we need a spiritual anchor that reminds us of God's love. We need to be reassured that God's care for us is like that of a nurturing mother: comforting, strengthening, and embracing. Even human sinfulness cannot dampen God's love. In fact, our weaknesses and failures are opportunities for us to grow closer to God, our divine Mother of Mercy who awaits us with open arms, assuring us of forgiveness and healing.

The awareness that God is always loving us can be a source of deep joy and peace. As Julian put it, "God is our true peace…and works to bring us into endless peace."[4] In the hectic pace of contemporary life, we often become distracted by the pressures that pull our focus away from the peace that is available in each moment. Julian showed us how to glimpse the inbreaking of grace in our relationships with others and in the world around us. Like Julian, we can be vibrantly alive to our present reality and find peace and joy in everything we do and in who we are—the beloved of God—loving self, others, and all creation.

As we enter the new millennium, soul sisters like Julian stir within our imaginations a new awareness of creation as a manifestation of the sacred in our midst. God, according to Julian, passionately loves our world just as God loves the hazelnut: "In this little thing I saw three properties. The first is that God made it, the second is that God loves it, the third is that God preserves it. But what did I see in it? It is that God is the Creator and the protector, and the lover."[5] Every blade of grass, every drop of water, every ray of sunshine, every flower, every tree, every rock, every tiny bug, every human person, is a reflection of the Lover of the Universe. Every living being reveals Creator Spirit within us and all around us. All of us are living words of God, revealing the beauty of the holy in our world. We have all been kissed by God and called to join in the cosmic dance of creation. Companions, like Julian, can help us discover the soul energy to birth this mystical vision that can connect us more closely with all other living beings.

Reflection

And so in our making, God almighty is our loving Father, and God all wisdom is our loving Mother, with the love and goodness of the Holy Spirit, which is all one God.... Thus in our Father, God almighty, we have our being, and in our Mother of mercy we have our reforming and restoring, in whom our parts are united and all made perfect...through the rewards and the gifts of grace of the Holy Spirit we are fulfilled.[6]

Discussion Starters

1. How can Julian's spiritual teachings on God's love change individual lives and the life of our society?

2. How is Julian a model of woman-wisdom for our time? What can contemporary women learn from her?

3. How can feminine imagery of God broaden our understanding of divinity and our understanding of ourselves as God's images?

4. How does Julian's understanding of the Trinity enlighten us?

Prayer Experience

(You may want to select classical or instrumental music to accompany this prayer.)

1. Begin by breathing in deeply through your nose and out through your mouth... Use your abdomen muscles to help you breathe deeply... As you breathe in, let go of all pressures that antagonize or distract you, and focus your awareness on peace and joy... Recite the following lines to help you do conscious breathing: "Breathing in peace... Breathing out joy..." or "Breathing in God... Breathing out Love..."

2. Reflect on the mother who gave you birth... Image God holding you close and loving you tenderly, just as your mother held you close and loved you tenderly... Feel the womb of God enfolding you with love...healing you...

3. Use this prayer for healing or create your own. Pray it slowly and mindfully: "O Nurturing, Nourishing, Mothering God, with you and through you I journey back to the womb that gave me birth... May you continue to delight in me... Heal the hurts that come from the

difference between the love I needed and the love I received... Reach deep within me as I rest in your womb... You, who loved me into existence and soothe away any pain or fear from my past, fill me with your life-giving force and creativity in my relationships with my parents, children, and all those I am called to nurture... I belong to you... I love you... I celebrate your birthing power within me that accepts me...that forgives me...that liberates me...in peace and joy forever..."

4. Be aware that Mother God is celebrating every moment of your existence, from your conception until now... Be aware that you can be a nurturer of your own life and creativity... Surround yourself with love... Surround your family, friends, and special people in your life, community, church, neighborhood, and world with love...

5. Write a love letter to yourself or do something to express the miracle you are. Consider smiling at yourself in a mirror, placing your hand gently on your heart for a few minutes, dancing, singing, being still, dreaming new dreams.

6. Write a love letter to someone special in your life with whom you have a nurturing relationship. Consider writing to your spouse, parents, children, grandchildren—or do something with one or more of these people to express your gratitude for the miracle they are. You might want to hold their photographs to your heart as you recall their specialness.

7. Create an affirmation, a positive message, to express God's nurturing love for you and/or your nurturing love for self or others. Repeat this brief phrase or sentence as often as you can. Consider using one of the following: "Mother God holds me close forever," "I am an amazing reflection of God's feminine face," "I experience

divinity within me," "I am strong and loving," "I love you," "You are my delight."

Sharing the Vision

6.

Catherine of Siena

Mystic Activist,
Lecturer of Popes

Caterina di Giacomo di Benincasa was born in 1347 in Siena, Italy. She was the twenty-fourth child of her parents, Monna Lapa and Jacopo. A happy, carefree child, Catherine enjoyed playing games. One of her favorite places was a beautiful staircase where she sat and observed much of the activity in her spacious home: her mother cooking delicious meals over the open hearth in the kitchen and the young apprentices making colorful dyes in her father's workshop. Moving up and down the steps, as small children do, Catherine recited Hail Marys, much the way girls today recite favorite rhymes as they jump rope.

Returning home one day with her brother, Stefano, from a visit with her married sister, Bonaventura, six-year-old Catherine had a vision near the church of Saint Dominic. She saw Christ, who looked directly into her eyes and smiled.

After this spiritual encounter, Catherine longed to be alone. On one occasion she even ran away to a little cavern on the edge of town, where she could pray by herself. At the age of seven, Catherine consecrated her life to God.

As a teenager, Catherine's austere—some would say, abnormal—behavior alarmed her family. She fasted, wore a tight iron chain around her waist, slept on a board, and regularly deprived herself of sleep. When she was fifteen she defied her parents' plans for her marriage and cut off her hair to ruin her appearance. In punishment, Catherine was assigned the menial household chores and was told that she had to share a room with her brother, Stefano. She was to be the family's servant and do whatever anyone asked of her. The goal, of course, was to make her life as miserable as possible so that she would marry as her parents had hoped.

Rather than resenting the way her family treated her, however, Catherine served willingly. She pretended that her father was Jesus, that her mother was Mary, and that her brothers and sisters were the apostles. Then one day her father called a meeting and told the family that Catherine would no longer have to live a life of drudgery. She would be left alone and would have her room to herself once again.

Thinking that a visit to a spa might help her daughter become "normal" again, Monna Lapa took Catherine to a resort near Siena. But Catherine stepped into water that was hot enough to scald her, leaving her with burns and blisters. Realizing that this treatment had failed, her mother gave up and they returned home.

Shortly after this fiasco, Catherine's father walked into the room where Catherine was praying and saw a white dove hovering over his child's head. This mystical event convinced him that Catherine's calling was genuine. He was so touched by this experience, in fact, that he allowed Catherine to give alms to the needy from family resources. Catherine's siblings soon discovered that if they did not keep their rooms locked, their valuables were likely to be given away.

Around this time Catherine became ill with smallpox. During this sickness, Catherine convinced her mother to support her plans of consecrating her life to God. Soon after her recovery, she joined the Mantellate, a women's group associated with the Dominican Order, who wore religious dress, lived in their own homes, and served the needs of sick and poor people. Her mother accompanied her to the ceremony in which she was clothed in the habit, and upon returning to their home, Catherine lived a life of deep prayer and solitude.

According to her biographers, Catherine lived like an anchoress, leaving her room only to attend Mass. She continued her bodily austerities, which included scourging her body, wearing a steel chain that chafed her skin, sleeping less than one hour a night, and engaging in severe fasts. When people expressed concern about her eating habits, Catherine would eat when she was being watched but would deliberately induce vomiting afterwards.

Some commentators think that Catherine's behavior was neurotic and unhealthy. Certainly her bulimic behavior, self-mutilation, and sleep deprivation are not to be recommended; not everything a saint does is to be imitated. However, it is important to understand that the reason for her self-inflicted physical torture was the belief that her penance would expiate her sins, the sins of those she knew, and the sins of the world. In other words, Catherine's motivation was love of God and love of neighbor.

It was not unusual, in fact, for saints during medieval times and throughout much of Church history to engage in severe bodily deprivations similar to those chosen by Catherine. Today spiritual directors would not recommend penances that harm the body, however. Instead, they would suggest a healthier approach that affirms the body as God's dwelling place. Fasting, for example, would be viewed as a valuable means to foster health in body and soul. Often people who fast choose to do so because they want to use less of Earth's resources, purify their bodies of toxins, and donate the money saved to feed hungry and homeless people.

Catherine had numerous ecstatic experiences. Christ appeared to her as a companion who walked with her and prayed with her. On one such occasion Christ spoke the following words: "Do you know, daughter, who you are, and who I am? If you know these two things, you will be blessed."[1] In another vision, Catherine experienced a mystical marriage in which Christ gave her a ring that could not be seen with the human eye but which Catherine claimed she always saw. One time, when Catherine prayed "for a clean heart," Christ came and took her heart with him. Several days later, he returned and gave her the divine heart, not hers. After this she experienced a profound love for other people. Christ also appeared standing outside

Catherine's door; he told her that she could serve God only by loving others. "The service you cannot do me you must render your neighbors....Your neighbors are the channel through which all your virtues come to birth."[2] As a result of that vision, Catherine finally left her room to join her Mantellate community, serving the sick, the poor, and the prisoners. She ministered in two nearby hospitals, nursing those ravaged with disease and comforting the dying. She also counseled prisoners.

Catherine became involved in the political and ecclesiastical controversies of her time. This included feuds between the papacy and the city-states, the return of the papacy to Rome, the reform of the Church, and the Great Schism—in which both Clement VII and Urban VI claimed to be pope at the same time. Traveling to Florence, Catherine tried to mediate peace between the city-states. In Avignon she advocated the pope's return to Rome, and in Rome she advised Urban VI, whom she had supported as the true Vicar of Christ. While she was in Rome, Catherine established a community of women who lived on charitable donations.

Catherine dreamed of a "papal council" that would heal and unify the Church. Not long after the meetings—that she had hoped would end the discord and divisions in the Church—she grew weary, however, and became so ill that she could not even drink water. Catherine died on April 29, 1380, at the age of thirty-three.

Catherine's love for truth as she understood it led her to take a strong stance for justice in the Church and society. She believed that justice is rooted in living the truth of God's love in harmony with self, others, and God. Scholar Suzanne Noffke observes that Catherine "was indeed a social mystic—but even more a mystic activist. Poverty, sickness, the suffering of injustice even to the point of death, were not merely evils or even systemic evils to her...they were that, and as such she fought them—but they were still mere pawns in the hand of the will of both oppressed and oppressor under God."[3]

Today more than ever we need to live with integrity, integrating prayer and action in our lives so that we can be effective instruments of truth and justice in our world. Prayer grounds us in the immensity of God's love. As we experience being loved deeply, passionately, totally, we become on fire with love for others—family, friends, neighbors, strangers. We become mystic activists, like Catherine, speaking out, taking risks, and doing whatever God calls us to do.

As a public figure and courageous prophet, Catherine was unafraid of speaking truth to people of power. In the midst of the chaos of Church politics and corruption, and despite criticism and opposition, Catherine spoke out. She reprimanded Pope Urban VI for silencing a friend of hers whose ideas she believed would have helped reform the Church: "Oh most holy father, be patient when people talk to you about these things. For they speak only for God's honor and your well-being... I know that your holiness wants helpers who will really help you—but you have to be patient enough to listen to them."[4]

Thousands of contemporary reform-minded Catholics around the world are attempting to dialogue with Church authorities about abuse of power, priority of conscience, lack of due process, violation of theologians' human rights in the institutional Church, women's exclusion from leadership positions, and a number of other critical issues. Before he died, Cardinal Bernadine started a common-ground initiative to foster dialogue among polarized groups in the Church. As in the fourteenth century, the Church at the dawning of the twenty-first century needs people who are open negotiators, respectful listeners, and courageous activists. The Church needs people who, like Catherine, seek reconciliation and healing. Perhaps today's Church needs to call a new council, one that will involve not just pope and bishops, but all God's people.

Raymond of Capua, Catherine's confessor, follower, and biographer, became one of her closest friends. In his account of her life, he recalls how Catherine changed the minds and hearts of many men who had initially opposed her. These men, in fact, often joined her circle of close friends.

On one occasion Raymond describes being healed by Catherine's prayers. When he returned to Siena with Catherine, to care for those who were dying of the plague, Raymond himself became ill with serious symptoms. He asked for Catherine's help and, after she touched his forehead and prayed for him, he recovered. Catherine's prayer expressed her hope that her "Very loved" Raymond would be permeated with the fire of "[Christ's] blazing charity."[5]

As good friends and partners in ministry, Catherine and Raymond are wonderful models of mutual support for women and men in the Church today. In the past thirty years more and more women have held pastoral positions with men. Although many have had wonderful experiences of partnership, some have experienced pain and conflict. There is much work to be done for women to be accepted as equal partners in ministry on every level—in the parish, the diocese, and the Vatican. Policies and systems of support need to be created, however, if this is to be realized. A wondrous outpouring of grace takes place when women and men, as soul friends, share prayer, develop relationships of mutual trust, and use their God-given gifts to work together for equality and justice for women in the Church. How many small faith communities can witness to this contemporary reality! As a friend to Raymond and many others, Catherine can inspire us on our way.

As a member of Sisters for Christian Community, I find Catherine of Siena a real soul sister with whom I can identify. This new form of religious life, founded in the 1970s, consists of persons who are committed to living an egalitarian gospel lifestyle that does not fit the present official, canonical categories. Catherine did in the fourteenth century what communities like SFCC are doing in the twentieth century: bonding together with women of like mind, living independently or communally as circumstances dictate, gathering for mutual support, and witnessing the gospel as mystic activists in our era. It is comforting to know that courageous women trailblazers have gone before us and have done similar things.

Catherine challenges us not to settle into a rut or become complacent. She inspires us to listen deeply, in the depths of our hearts, to God's call. She reminds us that our mission will involve not only comforting the afflicted but also afflicting the comfortable. When we hear the divine call we can go forth knowing that we are accompanied by great women like Catherine, who will be with us as we champion truth and justice and act as change agents for our Church and world. If not us, who? If not now, when? If not here, where?

Reflection

Letter 63
To Pope Gregory XI, at Avignon

In the name of Jesus Christ crucified and of gentle Mary
Dearest, most holy and gracious father in Jesus Christ,
    …You are in charge of the garden of holy Church. So [first of all] uproot from the garden the stinking weeds full of impurity and avarice, and bloated with pride (I mean the evil pastors and administrators who poison and corrupt the garden). Ah, use your authority, you who are in charge of us! Uproot these weeds and throw them out where they will have nothing to administer! Tell them to tend to administering themselves by a good holy life. Plant fragrant flowers in this garden for us, pastors and administrators who will be true servants of Jesus Christ crucified, who will seek only God's honor and the salvation of souls.…

Ah, what a shame this is! They ought to be mirrors of freely chosen poverty, humble lambs, giving out the Church's possessions to the poor. Yet here they are, living in worldly luxury and ambition and pretentious vanity a thousand times worse than if they belonged to the world! In fact, many layfolk put them to shame by their good holy lives.…. For ever since the Church has paid more attention to the material than to the spiritual, things have gone from bad to worse.[6]

Discussion Starters

1. Catherine called Pope Gregory XI to reform the Church. What reforms are needed in the Church today?

2. If you could have a private audience with the pope or leaders of your church, what issues would you talk about?

3. How are you working for renewal in the Church? What can you do to join with others in effecting reconciliation and healing in our Church today?

4. Who are the contemporary prophets who speak on behalf of truth and justice in the Church and the world? Are you one of them?

Prayer Experience

(Consider playing soft instrumental music for this prayer experience.)

1. Breathe in slowly through your nose and out through your mouth for a couple of minutes until you feel relaxed... As you inhale, breathe in the healing power of God... As you exhale, breathe out any fear, anxiety, or other blockages that keep you from experiencing God's love for you...

2. Simply be in God's presence...

3. If you become distracted, simply place the distraction in a balloon and let it float away... Use a prayer word such as "God," "Jesus," "Peace," or "Love" to help you be in God's presence...

4. Reflect on the Church... Think about your hopes and dreams for the people of God... Be aware of any feelings, images, thoughts, or insights that emerge...

5. Get in touch with the reforms that are needed in the Church if the gospel is to be proclaimed fully in our times... Imagine healing, reconciliation, and renewal taking place in the Church... Imagine what

that might look like...what it might feel like...what difference it might make.

6. See yourself as an instrument of love for the Church... Be aware of how God is calling you to speak truth to power...to work for justice...to build community...to advocate for reforms...Decide on one thing you can do, as an individual or with others, to help transform the Church... See yourself acting as if the Church is being healed...as if the Church is being reconciled...as if the Church is being renewed... Let your prayer be Christ's prayer: "That all may be one..."

7. Let your conscious breathing be your prayer for the Church... As you inhale, breathe in peace and justice for God's people... As you exhale, breathe out reconciliation and renewal for all God's people...for all creation... (Repeat this breathing prayer for as long as you can. It is powerful.)

Stretched
by the
Vision

7.

Joan of Arc

Champion of Conscience

Joan of Arc, patroness of France, was born in Domremy in Lorraine on June 6, 1412. When she was thirteen years old, she began to hear voices, an experience she shared with no one for several years. During this time, she turned down a marriage proposal and devoted her energies to prayer. These "special messengers," in particular Saint Catherine of Alexandria, Saint Margaret, and Archangel Michael, revealed that her mission was to deliver the French kingdom from English domination.

According to the terms of the treaty of Troyes, on May 20, 1420, the English king, Henry V, became King of France, ignoring the legitimate heir, the future Charles VII. The mental illness of Charles VI, French military defeats, and the alliance between England and Burgundy had laid the groundwork for this momentous upheaval. After the deaths of Henry V and Charles VI, the Duke of Bedford, regent of France for Henry VI, took on the task of routing the dauphin (Charles VII), who had fled beyond the Loire.

Orleans came under attack in 1428. Joan, after inviting others to join her and acquiring male clothing, a sword, a horse, and armed escorts, went to see the dauphin. After convincing Charles, along with his theologians and some of his court, of her mission, Joan led the Armagnac army in stopping the siege of Orleans. Joan, a young woman dressed in armor and known for her powerful prophecies, visionary experiences, and relationship with heavenly messengers, rallied a discouraged French army to victory.

In *Personal Recollections of Joan of Arc,* Louis de Conte recalls the conversation between Charles and Joan after the Orleans victory: "Joan, my frank, honest General, will you name your reward?... You shall quarter the crown and the lilies of France for blazon, and with them your victorious sword to defend them—speak the word." Joan replied, "Ah, I cannot, dear and noble Dauphin. To be allowed to work for France, to spend one's self for France, is itself so supreme a reward that nothing can add to it—nothing. Give me the one reward I ask...march with me to Rheims and receive your crown." The dauphin rose, held up his sword, brought it slowly down on Joan's shoulders, and said, "Ah, thou art so simple, so true, so great, so noble—and by this accolade I join thee to the nobility of France, thy fitting place! And more! more! To distinguish thy house and honor it above all others, we add a privilege never accorded to any before in the history of these dominions: the females of the line shall have and hold the right to ennoble their husbands when these shall be of infe- rior degree.... Rise, Joan of Arc, now and henceforth surnamed *Du Lis,* in grateful acknowledgment of the good blow which you have struck for the lilies of France."[1]

With great courage, Joan charged ahead, led the troops to capture several towns, and then escorted the dauphin to Rheims where, in July 1429, he was crowned as Charles VII, King of France. Later, however, this national liberator was captured by the Burgundians at Campiegne. She was sold to the English, brought to Rouen, and put in a military prison, where she was guarded by English jailers. Eventually Joan was put on trial as a heretic and a witch.

In her testimony, Joan defended her voices and mystical experi- ences in the face of challenges from Church authorities.[2] Her trial and retrial took place between 1450–1456. Of the one hundred and three theologians commissioned by the theological faculty of the University of Paris to hear the case, all but eight were French. The

English, however, financed and controlled the proceedings. Whenever there was a possibility of clemency, the English protested.

Records of the proceedings indicate that only one or two of the male theologian inquisitors ever raised a doubt about the proceedings. When they did, they were thrown into jail or had to flee for safety. Joan's judges, however, did not entertain any serious doubts about the case. Although the retrial cleared Joan of heresy, it did not deal with her right to claim authority or authenticity for her divine messengers. Joan defied the powers of the Church and affirmed herself as a messenger of God, a proper instrument for God's word, certain of the validity of her own religious experience. The verdict was unanimous: Joan of Arc was to be burned at the stake as a heretic.[3] As W. S. Scott noted: "In the person of the Maid, the ecclesiastical world of her day saw (and saw clearly for the first time) a new figure, of whom they were rightly afraid—the figure of one who throughout her short life claimed the absolute validity of her own religious experience...above all else a God-inspired, God-intoxicated individualist."[4]

Church historians have had a hard time explaining the Church's position on Joan's death. George Tavard, author of *Woman in Christian Tradition,* believed the trial was a sham, so orchestrated by the English as to be nothing more than a facade. Critical of both the English and French motives, John O'Brien, another historian, never admitted Joan's rejection of Church authority. It is interesting to observe that even her canonization proceedings, while declaring Joan a saint, failed to recognize the main reason that she was condemned as a heretic.[5] In short, Joan was charged with rejecting the authority of the Church by neither admitting her visions to a priest nor requesting guidance or approval of her spiritual experiences. Joan had placed her faith completely in her own religious experience—demonstrating a spiritual independence that defied the power of the Church.[6]

Joan of Arc is a role model for contemporary women and men who live the Church's teaching on primacy of conscience and who sometimes face condemnation, censure, threats, and loss of jobs in the Church for advocating theological or moral positions that differ from the preferred theologies of Church hierarchy. Like Joan, these accused women and men are often denied a fair hearing or due process. Like Joan, prophetic persons today who challenge patriarchy and the corruption of power in Church and society trigger a profound fear in ecclesiastical and civic leaders, which often leads to nothing less than contemporary "witch hunts."

The Church has a tendency to condemn creative thinkers, daring visionaries, and innovative leaders, such as Galileo, Joan of Arc, Meister Eckhart, Teresa of Avila, and John Courtney Murray—only to herald them later for helping the Church develop new insights and directions. This happened to Joan of Arc; it happens in our time. Perhaps this can be a source of hope and consolation for those who suffer today.

As the saint of "heretics," Joan of Arc reminds us not to lose heart. She inspires us, rather, to listen to the "voice" of God deep within our beings, our consciences, and to follow its directives. This does not diminish the importance of reflecting on and understanding the teachings of the Church, of course. But if our conscience and Church teachings are in conflict, we must follow our conscience. If we are condemned for doing so, truth will prevail in the end. The Spirit will guide the Church on the path of wisdom and one day, as with Joan of Arc, the Church will call us "saint" for our faithful witness to the gospel.

While no longer burning people at the stake, Church officials today, as in Joan's time, still struggle to recognize the validity of women's spiritual experiences and admit women to all ministries in the Church. Until recently, in fact, the Church basically ignored women in the tradition. Church history and theology were male enterprises enunciated almost exclusively by males for males. In 1995 Pope John Paul II apologized for past injustices to women and called for equality for women in all areas of life, except ordination to priesthood. The National Conference of Catholic Bishops in the United States called for alternative ways in which women can exercise leadership in the Church. But the United States Leadership Conference of Women Religious observed in their 1996 study titled *Creating a Home: Benchmarks for Church Leadership Roles for Women:* "As long as jurisdiction (the power to govern) is tied to ordination, a very limited number of roles with authority will be open to women." They concluded that, "The relationship of jurisdiction to ordination creates a glass ceiling for women in the church."

Little by little women are gaining a voice and achieving visibility in their organized struggles for equality in the Church. According to the 1997 National Pastoral Life Center Study, women comprise eighty-two percent of the estimated twenty-six thousand lay people and religious who are employed as parish ministers. Yet only twenty-five percent of all top diocesan administrative positions were held by women, according to a 1994 National Association of Church Personnel Administrators Study (involving one hundred participating dioceses). It is obvious that, although progress has been made, a long road lies ahead for women to become partners and equals with men as ministers in the Roman Catholic Church.

Women can take heart, however. This movement appears to be part of a larger global struggle for justice and liberation for women in society. Women today are forming international networks to address issues that impact the quality of life of women, including their political, social, and spiritual empowerment around the world. The Women's Conferences in Cairo and Beijing are but two examples of gatherings of organizations that have met to design strategies to deal with these global challenges.

Like Joan of Arc, women today are standing up and speaking out about their experiences. Their prophetic voices are changing ecclesial and societal attitudes toward women around the world. Viva Joan of Arc, visionary of God, saint of "heretics," champion of conscience, and model for women and men of the twenty-first century!

Reflection

Excerpt from the trial of Joan of Arc:

Joan: First, as to that on which you admonish me for my good and for our Faith, I thank you and all the company also, as to the advice which you offer me, also, I thank you; but I have no intention of desisting from the counsel of Our Lord.

Judge: Will you refer yourself to the judgment of the Church on earth for all you have said or done, be it good or bad?

Joan: In case the Church should wish me to do anything contrary to the command which has been given me of God, I will not consent to it, whatever it may be.

Judge: If the Church Militant tells you that your revelations are illusions or diabolical things, will you defer to the Church?

Joan: I will defer to God, whose commandment I always do. I know well that that which is contained in my case has come to me by the commandment of God; what I affirm in the case is that I have acted by the order of God: it is impossible for me to say otherwise. In case the Church should prescribe the contrary, I should not refer to anyone in the world but to God alone, whose commandment I always follow.[7]

Discussion Starters

1. Why is Joan of Arc a role model for women and men who follow their consciences? What does primacy of conscience mean? Why is this teaching of the Church important?

2. Joan placed her faith completely in her own religious experience. How are women today claiming, proclaiming, and celebrating their religious experience as autonomous persons? How have feminist theological analysis and women's religious studies reclaimed women's voices in the tradition?

3. What strategies and personnel policies are effective in advancing the participation of women in decision making and ministry in the Church? Is the education of women for ministry positions subsidized at the same level as that of men?

4. The Church has a tendency to condemn innovative thinkers and prophetic leaders, only to herald them later for helping the Church develop new insights and directions. How did this happen to Joan of Arc? Can you name others who were first criticized and later praised by the Church for their thinking, writings, or witness? Can this be a source of hope and consolation for those who suffer today? Why?

Prayer Experience

1. Relax and become centered... Breathe deeply so that with each breath, your abdomen goes up and down... As you breathe in, feel the warm, moist air flowing through your nostrils and filling your lungs... As you breathe out, slowly release the air to the atmosphere...Breathe slowly like this for several minutes until you feel relaxed...

2. Once you have quieted yourself, reread the Reflection.

3. Imagine you are present during this exchange between Joan and the Church official. Choose to be Joan, the inquisitor, or one of the judges in the room. Be aware of the setting: the sights...the sounds...the temperature of the room... Look around the room at the different people... Listen to the words spoken... Pay attention to any feelings, thoughts, or insights that occur as you meditate on this scene...

4. Become aware of your leanings...your promptings...your intuitions...your spiritual experiences... Imagine yourself sharing these with others... Imagine some people affirming your insights and wanting to share more with you... Imagine others rejecting your ideas...labeling you...condemning you...

5. Observe how you feel... Experience your own inner strength... Imagine yourself responding to your critics out of your own passion for truth and justice... Be aware of the risks you are willing to take for your convictions...

6. Get in touch with your own religious experiences, visions, and inspirations... Ask for God's wisdom, Sophia's guidance, that you may live the integrity of your own convictions no matter what the cost... Reflect on that which is so important to you that you would give your life in defense of it...

7. Imagine yourself sharing your religious experiences, visions, and inspirations with Church and/or civil leaders... See yourself conducting an open, respectful, honest dialogue with one or more of them... Imagine yourself sharing your conscience convictions...listening to their responses...listening for any new understandings... new questions...new insights...being aware of fresh possibilities... Open yourself to Holy Wisdom... In response to what you imagine, express your thoughts and feelings in spontaneous prayerful affirmations such as "God alone, I always follow," "I serve God first," or "God is calling me to (name God's calling for you)."

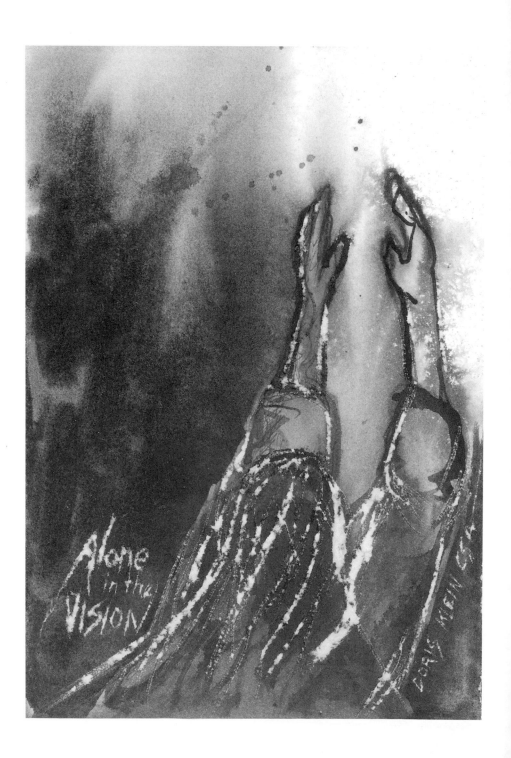

Alone in the VISION

DORIS KLEIN CSJ

8.

Teresa of Avila

Patron of Reformers, Teacher of Prayer

O n March 28, 1515, Teresa de Ahumada y Cepeda was born in the town of Avila in Castile, Spain. The third of twelve children, Teresa was the apple of her father's eye and a confidant to her mother. She wrote: "I was the most loved of my father." Because her mother was only twenty when Teresa was born, a close relationship developed between the two of them—a relationship that Teresa treasured. She remembered reading romantic tales of chivalry with her mother.[1]

At the age of eleven, Teresa experienced a heartbreaking loss when her mother died. She described her sorrow: "I remember that when my mother died I was a little under twelve. When I began to realize what I had lost, I ran crying to a statue of Our Lady and begged her to be my mother, with many tears."[2]

As an adolescent, Teresa was quite beautiful, charming, and often in love. She went out regularly with young suitors, frequently without her father's knowledge or permission. Teresa lied to her father about her affair with a man she hoped would marry her. Teresa recalled that her integrity was damaged when she was no longer a virgin, so "they put me in a convent in the neighborhood where they took care of girls like me, only not so evil in their ways."[3]

Nineteen months later, Teresa became ill with high fevers and fainting episodes. She was diagnosed as having heart problems and rheumatoid arthritis. At this time her father took her home, where she lived with her sister, Maria, and Maria's husband, de Guman. Theresa began reading the works of Saint Jerome and grew to fear that if she did not enter the convent she was destined for hell. When she pleaded to be allowed to enter religious life, Teresa's father initially refused but later gave his permission. Teresa explained that leaving home was a devastating experience: "I can remember completely what it was like, and in sober truth I don't think that the pain will be more when I die than when I walked out of my father's house, for I felt as if my very bones were being pulled apart."[4]

After entering the convent of the Incarnation in Avila in 1536, at the age of twenty, Teresa continued to care for her beloved father until his death: "I suffered much hardship during his sickness. I believe I served him somewhat for the trials he suffered during mine. Although I was very sick, I forced myself. Since in losing him I was losing every good and joy, and he was everything to me.... When I saw him coming to the end of his life, it seemed my soul was being wrenched from me, for I loved him dearly."[5]

After her father's death, Teresa lived in two worlds for nearly twenty years. On the one hand she longed for the intimacy with God that religious life offered her; on the other hand she was distracted by the pastimes that were part of convent living at the time. She found herself becoming attached to things that made her lose her focus on spiritual growth.

When she was forty years old, Teresa saw an image of Jesus in agony that changed her life: "The vision of Christ left upon me an impression of His most extraordinary beauty, and the impression remains today; one time is sufficient to make this imprint.... After I beheld the extraordinary beauty of the Lord, I didn't see anyone who in comparison with Him seemed to attract me or occupy my thoughts."[6] A tearful Teresa then told Christ that she would not rise from her prayer until he answered her plea—that she would not offend him again. From that time on, Teresa grew closer to Christ and developed a way of practicing the presence of God, which Teresa described as an intimate sharing between friends (*Autobiography* 8:5).

For Teresa, prayer became an ongoing conversation that freed her from the distractions that had preoccupied her during her early convent years. She could share everything—her joys, sufferings, failures, victories—with her beloved friend, God. On one occasion Teresa's wagon got stuck in mud as she was crossing a river. As she watched her supplies float away, Teresa heard God say to her: "This is how I treat my friends." "Then it's no wonder," she responded, "that you have so few!"[7]

Her deepening prayer life led Teresa to reform the Carmelite Order. For years she had ambivalent feelings about the lifestyle that she and other nuns were living. For example, the monastery often focused on social activities, such as entertaining wealthy young male patrons and advisees. Sometimes unhealthy liaisons developed; some nuns even became pregnant.

After prayerful reflection Teresa decided that it was time for a renewal of religious life. She would initiate communities in which the "primitive rule" would be followed, where women would live as passionate disciples of Christ through prayer and asceticism. Teresa believed that the fruitfulness of prayer was demonstrated in daily living. "What value God places on our loving and keeping peace with one another, the good Jesus places it before anything else."[8]

On August 24, 1562, Teresa opened Saint Joseph's Convent, the first of seventeen convents and four monasteries of Discalced Carmelites that she would found in the next twenty years. Discalced means "unshod"; the nuns wore sandals as a sign of their commitment to the "primitive rule" of the order. In spite of the opposition to these new communities from local people, clergy, and nuns, Teresa felt she was doing God's work. Nothing would stop her.

When Teresa wrote her *Autobiography,* she was under scrutiny for heresy by the Spanish Inquisition for her visions and raptures. If she had been convicted, she would been burned at the stake or would have suffered torture and condemnation, like many others. The Dominicans, who were in charge of the Inquisition, believed that theological knowledge was the only way one could know God. Thus they were suspicious of mental prayer, the prayer form that Teresa had introduced. It was not like the Latin prayer formulas used at that time, and posed an apparent threat to the authority of the Church. Fuente, one of her inquisitors, accused Teresa of misleading, evasive teaching: "She mixes falsehood with truth and water with oil.... And the water which is heresy, remains on the bottom, covered with the oil of truth. It will be necessary to stir these two liquids many times to uncover the concealed water, to discover the poisonous meaning that was underneath sweet words and spiritual language."[9]

Benedictine sister Joan Chittister thinks that the Inquisition confiscated Teresa's *Autobiography* because her prayer, ethnic identity, and reform agenda were a threat to Church authority: "Her prayer was too personal and...too Protestant.... She was hardly anti-Semitic enough since her father himself was Jewish; and she was starting something new."[10]

Teresa died at Alba de Tormes on October 4, 1582. In 1622 she was canonized by Pope Gregory XV and declared the first woman Doctor of the Church on September 27, 1970.

Teresa's writings include: *Autobiography, The Way of Perfection, The Foundations, Meditations on the Canticle, Visitation of the Discalced Nuns,* and *Interior Castle.* In her best-known work, *Interior Castle,* Teresa used the image of a castle to describe the seven "dwelling places" or stages of prayer. She wrote: "For if this castle is the soul, clearly one doesn't have to enter it since it is within oneself. How foolish it would seem were we to tell someone to enter a room s(he) is already in. But you must understand that there is a great difference in the ways one may be inside the castle" (1.1.5).

According to Teresa, the first three "dwelling places" show us how to let go of distractions and how to encounter the Holy One in meditation, spiritual reading, and good works. The fourth "dwelling place" is like a bridge between the natural and the supernatural, where we can "center" in the divine presence. The fifth is the prayer of union, in which the soul experiences life in Christ. The sixth is one of purification and transformation in preparation for total oneness with the divine. The seventh is complete communion with divine love.

Teresa was down to earth, practical, and determined. She was a visionary, a woman of passion whose energy can inspire us on our spiritual journey. She was a woman who loved life, knew her own sinfulness, felt the emptiness that God alone could fill, and discovered abiding peace in the presence of God.

Teresa knew how to make God accessible to ordinary people. Her description of prayer as a conversation between friends, a communication that can take place anytime and anyplace, is something that most people can understand. Applying Teresa's teachings about prayer today, we can converse with God while we drive to work, load the dishwasher, stand in line at the bank, mow the lawn, or walk the dog. Teresa reminds us that God is everywhere and grace abounds in our lives.

Even though she herself experienced ecstatic visions, Teresa warns us that these are not important, that we do not need to seek them. Rather, the love we show our neighbor is a far more reliable indicator of the fruitfulness of our prayer. In other words, our prayer should lead us to good works, and good works should lead us to prayer.

Teresa had a cheerful disposition; she did not put up with "sour-faced saints" and she enjoyed play. She often entertained her sisters, instrument in hand, encouraging them to lighten up and share laughter with one another. Although she was a busy reformer with a big agenda, traveling the length of Spain creating a new form of religious life during the last twenty years of her life, Teresa had time for recreation and fun. She knew that what we accomplish is not as important as the love in our hearts. Perhaps we need more play time in our lives. Like Teresa, we too can experience a passion for God in our passion for life.

Teresa's words continue to inspire generations of spiritual seekers. Her "Bookmark Prayer" is one that we can use again and again to calm our nerves, center ourselves, and let go and let God be in charge of our lives. Then, as night follows day, wondrous things will happen—maybe even a vision or two of God's love that will sweep us off our feet! Teresa has left us, contemporary saints-in-the-making that we are, a sound prescription for holiness, one we can find if we talk and walk with God.

Reflection

Let nothing disturb you,
Let nothing frighten you,
Everything is changing;
God alone is changeless.
Patience attains the goal.
Who has God lacks nothing.
God alone fills all our needs.[11]

Discussion Starters

1. What can we learn from Teresa of Avila that will help us on our spiritual journey?

2. Teresa defined prayer as a conversation with God. How would you define prayer? How do you pray?

3. What question would you like to ask Teresa of Avila? How is Teresa a soul sister for modern women and men?

4. What does it mean to be a reformer in the Church and world today? What can we learn from Teresa about reforming an institution such as religious life and/or the Church?

Prayer Experience

1. Sit in a comfortable position and close your eyes. Relax your entire body, beginning with your head, face, and neck... Alternately tense the muscles in each of these areas and then relax them... Move

your neck in a circle several times... Alternately tense and relax your shoulders, arms, hands, and fingers... Alternately tense and relax your stomach, back, hips, legs, feet, toes...

2. Slowly reread Teresa's Bookmark Prayer, as if God is speaking these words directly to you... Repeat a word or phrase that touches you...

3. Become aware that God is your closest friend... Choose a special place to have a conversation with God... Go there in your imagination...

4. Listen as God speaks to you in the depths of your heart...

5. Talk with God as you would your best friend...

6. Open yourself to God's strength...to God's peace...to God's mercy...to God's wisdom...to God's justice... Spend time simply being with your friend... Be aware of any images, feelings, or insights that emerge... Record these, if you want, in your prayer journal.

7. Be aware of ways you can live as a reflection of God's strength... as a reflection of God's peace...as a reflection of God's mercy...as a reflection of God's wisdom...as a reflection of God's justice... Decide on something you can say or do that will show your love to others or make a change in yourself that will be a blessing to others. (Consider saying "I love you" to your spouse or children, doing an extra chore, running an errand, quitting a bad habit, or affirming another person's goodness or God-ness.) Decide on one way you can

love and reform the Church. (Consider getting involved in a grass-roots organization or movement, or start one in your local parish or diocese. Join a committee to create more inclusive liturgies, or invite Church leaders to include more women in leadership positions and on pastoral and diocesan boards and offices.) Let the Spirit lead you.

doubting
the Vision

9.

Louise de Marillac

Dreamer of Impossible Dreams

Louise was born to Marguerite Camus and Louis de Marillac on August 12, 1591 at Ferrieres-en-Brie near Meux, France. Louise was three years old when her mother died and her father remarried a widow who had four children. At three years of age and feeling slightly lost in the shuffle, Louise was sent to be educated by her aunt, a Dominican nun at the Convent of Saint Denis at Poissy. There she received a classical education, including instruction in Greek and Latin. Louise later left the convent and studied under the direction of her scholarly father.

Louise suffered another great loss at the age of thirteen, when her father died. From then on she boarded with a woman who instructed her in the domestic skills of cooking, sewing, and household chores. During this time Louise began to express a desire to become a nun, and approached the Daughters of the Passion, also known as the Capuchinesses. She was rejected, however, for health reasons. Pere H. de Champagny, her spiritual director, advised her to marry.

So in 1613, Louise married Antoine Le Gras, an official in Queen Marie de Medici's court. Her marriage was happy and, within a year, a son was born to the couple. Louise was a wonderful wife and mother. For many years she enjoyed the companionship of her husband and the task of nurturing her child, while devoting much of her time to works of charity. She nursed her husband through a long and debilitating illness that eventually ended in his death on December 21, 1625, leaving Louise with a twelve-year-old son to raise alone.

Soon after her husband's death, Louise moved to a smaller house on the Rue Saint Victor, near Notre Dame, closer to her son's school and in the district where Vincent de Paul, her spiritual director, lived. Motivated by her love for the poor and sick, Louise joined Vincent in works of charity.

In May 1629, Vincent invited Louise to Montmirail, where he was in the process of establishing a mission. Louise's assignment was to assess the local lay volunteer organization that ministered to the poor and sick. This group, comprised mainly of women, came to be known as the local "charity." Louise started to direct the "Ladies of Charity" in the work of caring for the neglected members of society.

In 1633, Louise set up a training center in her own home for candidates interested in this work. After her success in that endeavor, Vincent asked her to travel to other parish charities to train their volunteers. By word and deed, Louise impressed the local charities with her willingness to visit the meanest hovels to clean, cook, and care for the sick and poor.[1]

On one of these trips Louise met Marguerite Naseau, a young peasant woman who had taught herself to read and was teaching others as well. Marguerite wanted to go to Paris to help Louise and Vincent in their ministry to the poor. After consulting together, they agreed that Marguerite's vocation was authentic. Soon after Marguerite arrived in Paris, she was joined by four other women who became known as Louise's "little company." Living in Louise's home, this small group of women committed themselves to the common life as lay persons.

Several months later Louise introduced a rule that included an hour of prayer each day. Also, the group met every Sunday for a spiritual conference given by Vincent, while Louise gave instruction to the members in nursing and care for the sick. This was the beginning of the Sisters (or Daughters, as Vincent preferred) of Charity.

For nearly twelve years Vincent and Louise acted as informal joint "superiors" of this group, but there was no plan to create a formal religious "order" at that time. The women who belonged to the community were piously engaged in the corporeal and spiritual works of mercy, "having no cloister but the fear of God, no religious habit but holy modesty."[2]

On March 25, 1634, after a year of training the ladies in her home, Louise dedicated herself to a life of charitable works. Other women joined her in this commitment and in May 1636, they opened La Chapelle Saint Denis, a large home near the residence of the Lazarist priests, who were founded by Vincent de Paul. Another house, opposite Saint Lazare, was established in 1641. This served as the mother house of the Sisters of Charity until the time of the French Revolution.

Louise was an intelligent and practical mentor who, with her sisters, provided the sick with proper nourishment and clean linens. They educated the poor regarding better ways to perform domestic chores, thus giving the poor a means of earning a living. They also offered the poor the teachings and values of the gospel. In every village the sisters trained catechists who would continue their work of religious education. Vincent de Paul described the sisters as angels who did the work of God on Earth, traveling from village to village, healing the sick, and proclaiming the Good News of salvation.

While the purpose of certain religious orders was to care for the sick in hospitals, Vincent and Louise's vision of their mission was to reach out and care for the sick and poor in their own homes. This often included doing the menial work in the home for those who were unable. A sister visiting a sick person, for example, would bring not only medical assistance but also compassionate love, sound instruction, and powerful witness to the entire family. The sisters got to know the family personally and became aware of its physical and spiritual needs, more so than if they had simply ministered to patients in a large, overcrowded institution. The Sisters of Charity contemplated and served Christ in the sick, poor, and neglected members of society.[3]

As the first women's community that did not live a cloistered, contemplative life, the Sisters of Charity made their commitment for one year at a time. Each woman promised "to apply myself all this year to the corporeal and spiritual service of the sick poor, our true masters, with the help of God, which I ask through His Son Jesus Crucified, and by the prayers of the Blessed Virgin. Signed _____ ."[4] The women wore ordinary clothes, their identifying garb being a gray dress and white head-covering.

Vincent was concerned that what had happened to his friends, Francis de Sales and Jeanne de Chantal, who founded the Visitation Order, would happen to the Sisters of Charity. The Visitation Order was established to serve the world, but the Church decreed that congregations of women must be cloistered. So the Visitation Sisters reluctantly conformed to this mandate and turned away from the original charism of the order. Louise and Vincent, however, were able to create a new paradigm for religious life, "unleashing a power latent in women to overwhelm the world with monumental good works."[5]

Louise and Vincent were pioneers in creating a community that provided a broad range of services for afflicted humanity. The Sisters of Charity were among the first, for example, to open soup kitchens in Paris, feeding hundreds and later thousands of destitute people on a daily basis. In their ministry, Louise and her sisters were compassionate channels of divine mercy. Everywhere they went they served the poor, counseled prisoners, visited the sick, and did countless other tasks to bring God's healing love to humanity.

In an unprecedented change, Vincent asked Louise to conduct retreats for noblewomen. This was a daring and innovative form of ministry for women in seventeenth-century France, since tradition had dictated that only male clerics gave retreats. But Vincent believed that Louise had much to share and would provide solid spiritual nourishment for the ladies of nobility—and she did.[6]

Vincent regarded Louise as a dear friend and spiritual companion. In one of his many letters to her he recounted some of his problems and then confided his trust in her: "All this is confided to your heart alone, and no other." Another time he admitted: "God alone knows, Mademoiselle, what He has done for me in giving you to me. In heaven you will know."[7]

By the time Louise died in 1660, the Sisters of Charity had grown to more than forty houses. Since then they have spread throughout the world and are found on five continents. Pope Pius XI canonized Louise de Marillac in 1934.[8]

Devoting herself to the poor, Louise was a heroic woman who ministered tirelessly to the sick and destitute members of society. She encountered the presence of God in each person she served, and her witness inspired other women to join her in this ministry. With Vincent de Paul, her spiritual companion, they changed the face of religious life in the Church. Since that time, for example, women no longer have to limit their choice to either the cloister or the contemplative life. Now they can be seen in neighborhoods, homes, soup kitchens, hospitals, orphanages, prisons — feeding the hungry, comforting the sick, counseling prisoners, teaching children, and doing whatever is necessary to bring the light of God's love to the world. Their prophetic vision challenges the Church to open itself to new possibilities for women in religious life. The Spirit is full of surprises!

Louise serves as a role model we can look to for inspiration as women in the modern Church explore alternative spiritualities and new forms of ministry. In our time a new paradigm for religious life seems to be emerging. Once again women and men are experimenting with new forms that transcend traditional religious boundaries. Some communities today, such as the Sisters for Christian Community, the Federation of Christian Ministries, certain women's groups, a host of small faith communities, and other new institutions, are embracing feminist values and living the gospel unencumbered by the institutional Church. They are pioneering a model of community in which the discipleship of equals is a reality. Many of these groups are not seeking status in the official Church; rather they simply live their vision with passion as explorers, innovators, and birthers of a new experience of church.

Today the Sisters of Charity are visible reminders of Louise's great legacy. All we have to do is reflect on the variety of services they continue to provide to the poor, sick, illiterate, and forgotten people in our midst. There is a great need now, as there was in

Louise's time, for Christians to live the gospel with boundless charity. This is the challenge of Christianity in every age.

Reflection

The origin of vows is found in the death of our Savior on the Cross.... It is the result of the promise He made figuratively when He said: "And I, if I be lifted up from the earth, will draw all things to myself!" Is not this promise, O my God, literally fulfilled in all those to whom Thou givest the grace of binding themselves by vows?... Thus all the actions of a person who has consecrated himself/herself to Thee, belongs to thee.[9]

The disposition of a soul which accepts with holy indifference whatever God wills in her regard is truly angelic, because the angels in Heaven destined to the guardianship of souls await peacefully God's orders...in order to communicate the holy inspirations that are necessary to men (and women) for their salvation.[10]

I have not left myself time to speak of the most heroic period in the life of Saint Louise, when for five years civil war was raging in France and all the evils of that troubled generation were multiplied; when battles were taking place in the provinces and soldiers were dying of wounds or starving to death...when food became scarce and prices so high that the shops closed; when the populace was starving and smallpox was making frightful ravages; when 100,000 beggars organized themselves in a body and nearly became the rulers of the Capital; when government almost yielded the scepter to anarchy. As misery mounted, Louise de Marillac rose too, although during this period, she was in continual ill health. She hurried where the need was greatest.... In Paris, she exhausted herself in trying to minister to all the unfortunates, to the soldiers, to the frightened girls and women and nuns who appealed to her aid, to the hordes of poor, and even to some of the organized beggars; nor did she forget the most wretched of all, those whom she had labored among for years, the criminals who were condemned to prison and to convict ships. But I cannot enumerate all her labors. If Saint Vincent received at this time the official title of Grand Almoner of France and was called the Father of his Country, surely an equivalent honor was due to Saint Louise.[11]

Discussion Starters

1. What impact do you think Louise de Marillac's ministry to the poor can have on the Sisters of Charity today? on the poor? on social service ministers? on you?

2. Louise and Vincent were close friends and spiritual companions. How can women and men who experience mutuality in relationships help one another grow in their spiritual lives? Have you ever experienced this kind of relationship? If so, did you grow? Describe your experiences.

3. Louise and Vincent created a new form of religious life. What new forms or paradigms of religious life and/or Christian community are emerging today? What impact do you think they may have on the twenty-first century? What impact do you think they will have on the institutional Church?

4. "Vincent received the official title of Grand Almoner of France, and was called the Father of his Country." Do you agree with Rev. John Fenlon that Louise deserved an equivalent honor? Why? Why are heroic women often ignored in the Church? in society? How can this be changed?

Prayer Experience

(You may want to play classical or instrumental music to accompany your reflection.)

1. Surround yourself with peace and tranquillity...

2. Reread the commentary and Reflection slowly and thoughtfully... Have a heart-to-heart conversation with Louise de Marillac about anything that her words or witness inspires in you...

3. Reflect on Louise and Vincent's close friendship and spiritual companionship... Reflect on intimate friendships in your life... Be conscious of ways these relationships helped you grow spiritually... Share your thoughts and feelings about these experiences with God...

4. Consider the new form of religious life that Louise and Vincent created... Imagine an exciting new form or paradigm of religious life and/or Christian community for our time... Be aware of any thoughts, images, symbols, and sensations that emerge...

5. Imagine yourself living this simple vision of religious life and/or Christian community... Imagine that you are an explorer...an innovator...a birther...of this new form or paradigm...Imagine others with you in this new community... Think of something wonderful that might happen... Imagine the changes...the challenges...the growth...the opportunities... Imagine others sharing these changes with you...

6. Open yourself to God's Spirit dwelling in the depths of your being... See yourself acting as if your vision of the Christian life is happening now... Draw an image or symbol of your experience.

7. Be aware of opportunities to serve the poor in your area... Ask God's Spirit to fill you with compassion, understanding, and wisdom... Ask God to guide you to respond in some concrete, practical way, such as serving in a soup kitchen, working at a shelter for those who are homeless, spending time with patients who have AIDS, answering phones at a rape crisis center, taking hot meals to those who are homebound, tutoring a child with learning disabilities...

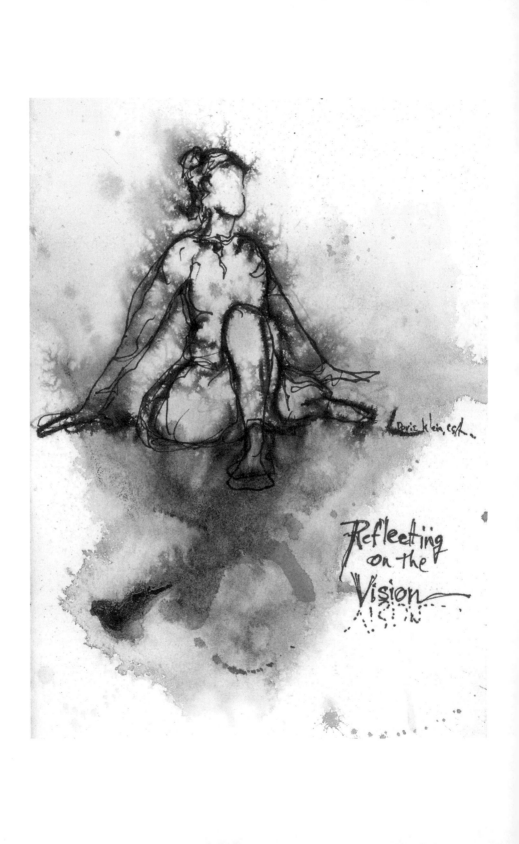

Doris klein, csj.

Reflecting
on the
Vision

10.

Sor Juana Ines de la Cruz
Mentor of Woman-Wisdom

Juana Ines Ramirez de Asbaje was born on November 12, 1648, in the village of San Miguel, Mexico. Juana and her two sisters were raised by their mother on their grandfather's ranch; Juana never knew her father. By the age of three, Juana already displayed a great love of books and begged her older sister to teach her to read. By the age of six, she could read and write. She pleaded with her mother to allow her to dress in boy's clothes so that she could attend the university, since only boys and men customarily attended school. Naturally her mother refused, so Juana spent a great deal of time in her grandfather's library reading as many as books as she could. When she thought she was not learning quickly enough, she cut her hair short.[1] She believed that if she didn't have the beauty of wisdom, she would not allow herself to have the beauty of hair.[2]

Juana's grandfather died when Juana was approximately nine years old. Soon after, Juana moved to Mexico City to live with her wealthy uncle and aunt: Juan de Mata and Dona Maria. In their care, Juana had new opportunities and learned much more than she ever could in her grandfather's library.

Juana lived with her aunt and uncle until she was fifteen, when she was admitted to the viceroy's court. Leonor Carreto, the viceroy's wife, took a liking to Juana and invited her to live in the palace as one of her attendants. The two women became close companions and enjoyed discussing art, literature, and music. When Juana began writing poetry, Leonor affirmed and supported her work as much as she could. Juana indicated her appreciation of Leonor's role in her life in a sonnet she wrote on the death of her patron and friend: "Unhappy lyre whereon your music played...."[3]

Juana enjoyed concerts, plays, dances, and other activities that were part of court life, and made frequent reference to palace balls and parties in her poetry. One time the viceroy invited forty men— philosophers, mathematicians, and poets—to dialogue with the fifteen-year-old young woman. They were all amazed at her intelligent comments and learned answers. Calleja, her biographer, describes her as surrounded by "the refined aura of flattery."[4]

Even though she was beautiful, charming, and intelligent—and probably had many suitors—Juana never married. During this era marriages were arranged between the heads of families, and a dowry, of course, was a key issue in these negotiations.[5] These marital arrangements implied some kind of financial and/or material contribution on the part of the bride's family. Some scholars believe that Juana did not marry an educated man with similar interests because she virtually had no family and thus no dowry.

Juana entered the Hieronimite Convent of San Jeronimo, known for its moderate discipline, and took her vows and the name Sor Juana Ines de la Cruz on February 24, 1669. At the time of her entrance, a wealthy man, Pedro Velazquez de la Cadena, paid her dowry. Some experts believe that a combination of circumstances contributed to Juana becoming a nun: her illegitimacy, poverty, and the absence of a father. Calleja explains her situation: "The good countenance of a poor woman is a white wall every fool wants to foul."[6] In her own writings, Sor Juana herself explained her motivations for choosing religious life: "And so I entered the religious order, knowing that life there entailed certain conditions...most repugnant to my nature; but given the total antipathy I felt toward marriage, I deemed convent life the least unsuitable and the most honorable I could elect if I were to ensure my salvation." Juana admits that her desire to live alone and to be able to freely engage in her studies without outside interference were important influences in her decision to become a nun. This was not unusual; the majority of nuns and monks at this time chose the cloister as a career or profession.[7]

The convents in Mexico City at the end of the seventeenth century were cultural and religious centers. In fact, the religious establishments of the day resembled modern corporations. The convents had "cells" that were rented or sold to the nuns. Their population consisted of nuns, maids, lay sisters, and "girls"—children whose parents had put them in the care of the nuns. There were three maids for each nun, although some convents had five maids per nun.[8] Juana's quarters consisted of a bedroom, bathroom, kitchen, and living room. She also had a large collection of books, art, and scientific and musical instruments, and was able to spend most of her time studying and writing.

Sor Juana had many visitors including writers, world travelers, and scientists. She impressed them all with her knowledge and intelligence, conversing in different languages as required. She was witty and gay and thoroughly entertaining. Although she could compose poems spontaneously, she often wrote her poetry to celebrate certain occasions, setting her words to music and playing them on instruments from her own musical collection. In addition to poems, Juana wrote songs and plays, all of which contributed to her widespread reputation. During the twenty-seven years she spent in this convent, she would became known as a great writer of Spanish poetry.[9]

On one occasion Sor Juana became involved in a dispute between two Church leaders. The bishop of Puebla asked Sor Juana to write a letter criticizing a sermon that had been written by Father Antonio Vieyra forty years earlier. The bishop hoped that Sor Juana's letter would anger the archbishop, who was a supporter of Father Vieyra. Sor Juana obediently wrote the letter. So that the archbishop would not suspect that the introduction had been penned by one person and the letter had been written by someone else, the bishop wrote an introduction to the letter under the pen name of a nun, "Sor Filotea."

As predicted, the criticism of Vieyra's sermon aroused the wrath of the archbishop. In her popular work, "Response to Sor Filotea de la Cruz," Sor Juana affirmed her interest in the intellectual life and declared that "women should be able to study, think, and write."[10] She also advocated the rights of women to write, study, and discuss ideas. She pointed out that the Church permitted women saints to write— women such as Santa Gertrudis, Santa Teresa, and Santa Birgitta, as well as women who were not saints, such as the Nun of Agreda and Sor Maria de la Antigua. Juana proposed that "Saint Paul's prohibition that women keep silence in the church is…directed solely to the public office of the pulpit, for if the Apostle had forbidden women to write, the Church would not have allowed it."[11]

Sor Juana's advocacy of women's rights exacerbated the archbishop's already deep-seated misogyny. He admitted that "if a woman even entered his house, he would have the bricks she stepped on removed. He thanked God that he was nearsighted so that he wouldn't have to see women."[12]

During this period there was a great shortage of food, and people rioted in desperation. The archbishop provided assistance to the people so that they could survive this crisis, thereby increasing his own favor and influence. Taking advantage of his enhanced standing, the archbishop used his power to try to silence Sor Juana. In the end, after a long contest, Juana gave up the struggle, stopped writing, and surrendered her books. On March 5, 1694, Sor Juana signed a document that reflected her submission to Church authority.

This document conveyed three distinct thoughts: the first paragraph reaffirmed Sor Juana's belief in the dogmas of the Roman Catholic Church; the second requested forgiveness, although none of her offenses were mentioned; the third reaffirmed the promise she had made to believe in Mary's Immaculate Conception. She concluded with a dramatic gesture: "And as a sign of how greatly I wish to spill my blood in defense of these truths, I sign with it."[13]

Scholars find it strange that the declaration contained no mention of a renunciation of literary pursuits. More mysterious yet, the original document has disappeared. Octavio Paz observes: "It is difficult to believe that the self-confident and defiant person of 1691 and 1692 had turned into the raving penitent of 1694.... I have no doubt that she defended herself to the last and refused to sign an abdication and nullification of her entire life. The purpose of the title superimposed by Castorena is to prove that the long process that had begun with the admonitions of Nunez de Miranda...had ended with a spectacular abjuration."[14]

An epidemic broke out shortly afterward, and Sor Juana died on April 17, 1695, while caring for her sisters. Calleja described her final days: "The illness was extremely contagious and Sister Juana, by nature compassionate and charitable, attended all without rest and without fear of their proximity."[15]

As one of the great Latin American poets, Sor Juana—her life and her poetry—enriches the imagination and stimulates the intellect. In a society that is still struggling with equal rights for women, Juana stands out as a role model. To her, reason knew no gender and intelligence was not restricted to men. As a seventeenth-century feminist, Sor Juana would feel at home in our contemporary Western society, where women are not defined or limited to any one role, but are free to live their full God-like potential. Her story reminds women of all ages to take time for personal development and intellectual pursuits. As an advocate of universal education for women in their own homes or in institutions, Juana is a mentor for women who are illiterate, women who are scholars, and all those women who today pursue learning for its own sake.

Like Sor Juana, women today face condemnation and censure by Church authorities who fear the power of women. Yet there are courageous women who advocate women's rights no matter how Church officials threaten them. Sor Juana's story reminds us to persevere even if there are moments when we weaken or feel like giving up. Perhaps that is the meaning of Juana's defeat by Church authorities. Sometimes light breaks forth in the darkest moments.

An example of this is Pope John Paul II's statement entitled "Letter to Women." For years women have been calling for the transformation of patriarchy and an end to gender discrimination in the Church. The Vatican seemed not to be listening. Then, on July 10, 1995, Pope John Paul II released a letter to the women of the world regarding "the great process of women's liberation." The pope apologized for the historical conditioning that has caused "an obstacle to the progress of women." Women have been relegated to the margins of society "and even reduced to servitude.... If objective blame, especially in particular historical contexts has belonged to not just a few members of the church, for this I am truly sorry." The pope went on to praise the women's movement: "I cannot fail to express my admiration for those women of good will who have devoted their lives to defending the dignity of womanhood by fighting for their basic social, economic and political rights, demonstrating courageous initiative at a time when this was considered extremely inappropriate." In its apology to women for the persistence of sexism in society, including the Church, and in its recognition of the positive contributions of the women's movement, this letter was a clear departure from previous Vatican statements by the pope.[16]

Some critics were astounded that the pope used the qualifier "if" in his apology. Many had hoped that Pope John Paul II's letter would include: an admission that the Church is living in the sin of institutionalized patriarchy; an appeal for forgiveness for damages and wounds that have been inflicted on women and men by this sinful condition; and a promise to take action to transform, heal, and change patriarchy now. It remains to be seen if the words of this letter are supported by actions to change the status quo, or if this was merely another instance of paying lip service.

At the order's Thirty-fourth General Congregation in 1995, the Jesuits issued their document titled "The Situation of Women in Church and Civil Society." The statement challenged Jesuits "to listen carefully and courageously to the experience of women" and "to align themselves in solidarity with women."[17]

As more and more women share their hopes, dreams, and visions, and network with one another from different religious, cultural, ethnic, and racial backgrounds, a brand new world is being born. Women today are making their voices heard in global decision making. The Cairo and Beijing Women's Conferences are two recent international meetings at which women exercised their political power and expressed their professional expertise on a wide range of issues, such as women's priorities in health, education, environmental safety, and peace and justice issues.

Can you imagine Sor Juana representing Mexico at these conferences and sharing her ideas for the future of our world and our Church? Wouldn't that be interesting? Do you belong to a women's group or mixed-gender community that gathers together to focus on justice and equality for women in Church and society? If not, join one or start one.

Reflection

I confess, too, that though it is true, as I have stated, that I had no need of books; it is nonetheless true that they have been no little inspiration, in divine as in human letters.... Without mentioning any infinity of other women whose names fill books, for example, I find the Egyptian Catherine, studying and influencing the wisdom of all the wise men of Egypt; I see a Gertrudis studying, writing and teaching. And not to overlook the examples close to home, I see my most holy mother Paula, learned in Hebrew, Greek, and Latin, and most able in interpreting the Scriptures....

I would want these interpreters and expositors of Saint Paul to explain to me how they interpret that scripture. Let the women keep silence in the church. For either they must understand it to refer to the material church, that is the church of pulpits and cathedrals, or to the spiritual, the community of the faithful, which is the Church. If they understand it to be the former, which in my opinion, is its true interpretation, then we see if in fact it is not permitted of women to read publicly in church nor preach, why do they censure those who study privately? And if they understand the latter, and wish the prohibition of the Apostle be applied transcendentally—that not even in private are women to be permitted to write or study—how are we to view the fact that the Church permitted a Gertrudis, a Santa Teresa, a Santa Birgitta, the Nun of Agreda, and so many others, to write?...In which case, Saint Paul's prohibition was directed solely to the public office of the pulpit, for if the Apostle had forbidden women to write, the Church would not have allowed it.[18]

Discussion Starters

1. How was Church hierarchy for and against Sor Juana? How is Church hierarchy for and against women today?

2. In his unprecedented "Letter to Women," Pope John Paul II apologized to women for the persistence of sexism in human society, including the Church, and recognized the positive contributions of the women's movements. How is this significant?

3. The pope's document reflected with women on the problems and issues of what it means to be a woman today. The Jesuit document does not propose to make such a claim, stating "We do not pretend or claim to speak for women." Rather the document invites "all Jesuits to listen carefully and courageously to the experience of women." What is the difference between these two approaches? In light of these documents, can men determine women's roles? What can you do to heal sexism and change patriarchy now?

4. Sor Juana was an intellectual giant and advocate of women's rights born ahead of her time. What questions and issues would she raise if she were alive today?

Prayer Experience

1. Be aware of your breathing... As you inhale, breathe in the Wellspring of Wisdom... As you exhale, breathe out the Source of Your Liberation... As you inhale, breathe in Sophia, Woman of

Strength and Knowledge... As you exhale, breathe out understanding...breathe out insight...breathe out wisdom...

2. Slowly and thoughtfully, reread the commentary and Reflection. When a thought, feeling, or image impresses you, stop and let it develop within you... Dialogue with Sor Juana... As you do so, be aware of any new understandings, images, or insights that emerge...

3. Reflect on Sor Juana as a mentor for women today who want to live their full God-like potential... Become aware of your interests in intellectual pursuits... If you could do so, what ideas, studies, hobbies, reading, writing, poetry, etc. would you pursue? Consider some exciting new possibilities that you might want to explore...

4. Invite Sophia, Wellspring of Wisdom, to reveal to you any new ideas, insights, or images that will help you become holy and more integrated in your life...

5. Reflect on the following two insights in Pope John Paul II's unprecedented "Letter to Women": he apologized to women for the persistence of sexism in society, including the Church, and he praised the positive contributions of the women's movement. Be aware of any questions that you would like to ask the pope... Share with Sophia, the Wellspring of Wisdom, your thoughts and feelings about women's equality in the Church or society... Pray for healing of sexism and transformation of patriarchy in Church and society... Record your insights, feelings, images, or thoughts in a journal, or express them in poetry, art, song, dance, or in some other creative way.

6. Imagine you have been asked to join an international committee of women whose task is to draft a document on women in the Church.

Imagine who the other women are who will work with you on this document... Imagine how you will begin... Consider the processes you will use to reflect on women's experiences... Imagine how you would define the situation... Ask Sophia, Wellspring of Wisdom, to accompany you on this journey... Dialogue with Sophia and other women about the experiences that women encounter in their struggle with patriarchal structures in the Church and society... Listen to the Wellspring of Wisdom as she reveals to you places of new life...sources of liberation...dynamic energy for empowerment ...hidden gifts of women... Listen to Sophia as she introduces you to women mentors from the Scriptures and tradition who want to share their experiences of oppression and empowerment...

7. Now imagine the document is finished... Your "Letter to Women" has involved women from every nation... It is unprecedented... It is new... It is exciting... It is energizing... It is empowering... Observe women everywhere affirming...welcoming...and celebrating its message... Now take some time to reflect on your journey... Focus on any new discoveries that surprised you...that encouraged you...that challenged you... Imagine how some men in the Church hierarchy today will condemn this document... See yourself and the other women meeting with Vatican officials... Hear these officials threatening to take punitive measures against you... Imagine how you and the other women respond to them... Then imagine something unexpected happening... Note your response in a journal, or express yourself in poetry, dance, song, art, or some other creative way.

Embracing the
Vision

11.

Kateri Tekakwitha

Icon of Integrity

Kateri Tekakwitha was born in 1656 in the Iroquois village of Ossernenon—now Auriesville, New York. Kateri's mother, a Christian Algonquin who was raised among the French at Three Rivers, was kidnapped back by the Iroquois and was married to a Mohawk chieftain of the Iroquois nation. They had two children—a daughter, Kateri, and a son. The family, however, was torn apart by disease and death when Kateri was four years old; her mother, father, and brother died in a smallpox epidemic. Although Kateri survived the disease, her face was left badly scarred and her eyesight damaged. Her uncle, an important tribal leader, adopted her.

In 1667 Kateri had her first encounter with missionaries when three Jesuits arrived at Caughnawaga. They were sheltered at Kateri's uncle's residence, and she was given the responsibility of providing them care and hospitality. Although she did not express an interest in becoming a Christian, Kateri was moved by the priests' gentle and devout witness to the gospel in their daily routines. "As it was, she stole silently out of the lodge in the dusk of evening to bring water for the simple Indian repast she was preparing for her guests, and all the while her thought was alive with God—the God she had never known...this Rawenniio, this true God was everywhere."[1] Scholars speculate that Kateri's initial reticence to the Christian faith was due to fear of her uncle, who opposed the spread of this new religion in the Mohawk villages.

Kateri's family intended for her to marry a young man from the Iroquois tribe. Both families being amenable to the match, arrangements were made for the young man to enter her cabin and sit beside her. In the "Letter and Life of Katharine Tekakwitha," Father Cholenec described Kateri's response to this matchmaking effort: "Tegahkouita (Tekakwitha) appeared utterly disconcerted when she saw the young man seated by her side. She first blushed, and then rising abruptly, went forth indignantly from the cabin; nor would she re-enter until the young man left it." Angered by her refusal to consider this young Iroquois for marriage, the family ostracized Kateri and treated her as a servant, "obliging her to do everything most painful and repulsive, and maliciously interpreting all of her actions, even the most innocent."[2]

One day in the autumn of 1675 Kateri was home alone. She was recovering from a foot injury and had not been able to attend the harvest with the other women. As Father Jacques de Lamberville past by her lodge, an unexplainable impulse moved him to visit. Inside the lodge he found Kateri who, seizing the opportunity, fervently expressed her desire to become a Christian: "The ardor with which she spoke, the courage she evinced, and a certain air, at once modest yet resolute, which appeared on her face, proved to the missionary that...God had great designs upon her soul."[3] Lamberville immediately accepted her as a catechumen and began her instruction in the Christian faith.

Kateri was baptized on Easter Sunday, April 5, 1676. On this momentous occasion, the Christians of Caughnawaga decorated the chapel with beaver and elk skins, brightly colored bear-skin rugs, buffalo hides, wampum belts, and beautiful shrubs and wildflowers. The people observed the ceremony attentively and, when it was over, Kateri seemed "bright with angelic joy. The Mohawks could almost believe they were looking at a blessed spirit rather than at one of themselves. The choir of Indian children...now filled the chapel with joyous melody, and made it resound with the sweet words of an Iroquois hymn."[4]

Some members of Kateri's tribe could not accept her conversion and made every effort to cause difficulty for her. They insulted her, deprived her of food, and dispatched boys to throw stones at her when she went to the chapel. Some even threatened her life. Some of the children joined in the derision by mocking her and calling her "Christian" with as much disdain as if they were calling her a dog. Yet Kateri remained resolute and said that she would rather die than abandon her Christian faith.[5]

When Kateri could no longer take the abuse, she fled with three warriors to a Christian village on the St. Lawrence River near Montreal. In October 1677 the fugitives completed their two-hundred-mile journey through the wilderness to the Mission of Saint Francis Xavier at Sault Saint Louis. There Kateri lived in a house with an adopted sister, also a Christian who had sought refuge at the mission. The house was under the guidance of Anastasia Tegonhatsihongo, a mentor and spiritual mother to the young women.

In her first months there, Kateri exhibited great fervor. People observed that she "knows only two paths, the path to the fields and the path home; she knows only two houses, her own home and the 'church.'"[6] Impressed by Kateri's spiritual progress, the priests in charge of the mission made an exception to their practice of waiting several years after baptism before giving a new Christian First Eucharist. Consequently on Christmas Day of 1677, Kateri was permitted to receive Holy Communion for the first time.[7]

In the winter of 1677–78, Kateri went on the traditional winter hunt. She would get up early to help prepare breakfast for the hunters and participate in the morning devotions, which were prayed in common. Then, when there was nothing in particular happening, she would walk into the woods, to the tree on which she had marked a cross, for solitary prayer.

On one occasion during this hunt, a woman accused Kateri of having sexual relations with her husband. The woman insisted that she had found her husband asleep one morning not far from Kateri's place in the lodge. The hunter, the story goes, came in late, exhausted from a long chase after a Canadian elk, and fell asleep in the first spot he found. The accusation was investigated, and Kateri was found innocent of the charge. Before the hunting party returned to the village, however, another woman expressed suspicion about Kateri's relationship with her husband.

Kateri suffered deeply from these accusations: "What grieved her was that the Father seemed not to believe her, and accused her as if she had been guilty; but God permitted it thus to purify her virtue.... She said only what was necessary to make known the truth, and said not the least thing that could make it appear that she was displeased with any one of those who were with her at the chase."[8]

Kateri had the opportunity to observe the manner and way of life of nuns she encountered in Montreal. She was especially impressed by their commitment to God, and decided that she, too, wanted to consecrate her life to God as a Christian virgin. "While passing some days at Montreal, where for the first time she saw the nuns, she was so charmed with their modesty and devotion that she informed herself most thoroughly with regard to the manner in which these holy sisters lived, and the virtues which they practiced." Kateri consulted with her spiritual director and asked permission to make a vow of virginity. Cholenec remembers: "She gave me no peace till I had granted her permission to make the same sacrifice of herself not by a simple resolution...but by an irrevocable engagement which obliged her to belong to God without any recall... I would not, however, give my consent to this step until I had...been anew convinced that it was the Spirit of God acting in this excellent girl, which had thus inspired her with a design of which there had never been an example among the Indians."[9] On March 25, 1679, Kateri made a vow of perpetual virginity.

During the years that followed her commitment to God, Kateri endured a great deal of suffering. She was frequently ill with severe headaches, high fevers, stomach pain, and nausea. In spite of these infirmities, however, she continued her generous service to the needs of others in the community and spent hours in daily prayer. Kateri also fasted on a regular basis and performed many acts of mortification. Her witness to the gospel was a source of inspiration to the whole village.

Two months before her death, Kateri became so ill that administration of the last rites was deemed necessary. On Tuesday of Holy Week, the Indians of the village accompanied the priest carrying the Eucharist to Kateri's cabin. Her friends wanted to be with her in her last moments, but Kateri assured them that they could leave to go about their daily routines.

On Wednesday, April 17, 1680, at the age of twenty-four, Kateri died in the peaceful embrace of her loving community. Fifteen minutes after her death, Kateri's face took on a special beauty and radiance that amazed all who were present. Two French colonists, who did not know that Kateri had died, commented: "See what a beautiful Indian girl is sleeping there!"[10] Kateri's death had an extraordinary effect on the Indian community. Many healings and miracles were reported owing to her intercession.

Kateri Tekakwitha, often referred to as the "Lily of the Mohawks," reminds us that ordinary people can achieve heroic holiness by doing the best they can to love God and love neighbor in the everyday circumstances of life. Kateri gave of herself, generously choosing to suffer discomforts in order to serve the needs of the community. In every adversity of life, she reacted with self-discipline and perseverance. Inspired by the boundless love God demonstrated by Jesus Christ on the cross, Kateri practiced acts of self-denial, such as fasting, in order to grow strong in the Christian life. As a courageous Native American woman, she defied tradition and chose celibacy in order to pursue more purely her passionate religious beliefs. For her this was a normal part of gospel living that strengthened her to love others even more deeply. When she was falsely accused of sexual misconduct, she told the truth and forgave those who maligned her. She met cruel treatment and humiliating jeers with a martyr's courage.

Kateri demonstrated that a Christian can witness to the gospel in the midst of pain, rejection, and suffering. As a Native American woman who lived simply, truthfully, and courageously, she challenges us to live Christian values with integrity, no matter what circumstances, opposition, or criticism we encounter.

Kateri leaves a rich legacy of spirituality that has inspired many people. Thousands of Americans have committed themselves to spreading Kateri's example by participating in the Tekakwitha League and the Kateri Guild. In this century, Indian tribes have presented the pope with thousands of signatures on petitions requesting Kateri's canonization. Today, more than three hundred years later, her radiance continues to glow, reminding us of the Creator's wondrous love and our human potential for holiness.

Reflection

You may take my life, but not my faith.[11]

I am not any longer my own, I have given myself entirely to Jesus Christ.[12]

I am going to die. Remember always what we have done together since we knew one another... Never give up mortification. I will love you in heaven,—I will pray for you,—I will help you.[13]

Discussion Starters

1. What insights does Kateri Tekakwitha's life reveal about living the gospel in our time?

2. What circumstances, events, and people challenge your faith now? What significance do they have in your spiritual journey?

3. What role does mortification or self-denial play in the Christian life? What opportunities do you have each day for this Christian practice?

4. What impact will your death have on the people you love?

Prayer Experience

1. Inhale deeply, slowly... Exhale deeply, slowly... Keep breathing this way for several minutes or until you feel relaxed...

2. Slowly and thoughtfully reread the commentary and the Reflection...

3. If possible, take a walk in a park, a wooded area, along a nature trail, or go to one of your favorite outdoor areas. If you cannot go outdoors, use your imagination to picture your favorite nature scene...Observe the sky...the clouds...the sun...the rain...the snow... the birds...the squirrels...the bugs...the dogs...the cats... Feel the warmth or coolness of the air... Listen to the sounds of Earth's creatures... Hug a tree... Lie on the grass... Caress an animal... Be attentive to Earth...

4. Open yourself to the powerful love of Creator God whispering a love song to you: embracing you in the music of trees swaying, longing for you in wind blowing, rising and setting for you in sun shining, dancing for you in snowflakes swirling, or crying for you in raindrops falling... Reflect on one or more of these images... Be aware of any sensations, feelings, intuitions, or insights that emerge... Record these, if you want, in your prayer journal, or express yourself in poetry, art, dance, song, or in some other creative way.

5. Reflect on how God is present with you in the ordinary experiences of life... Be aware that God dwells in you and you dwell in God... Recall the circumstances, events, and people that most challenge your faith... Ponder their significance in your spiritual journey...

Ask God to help you live the gospel without compromise, regardless of the criticisms...the abuse...the risks...

6. Be conscious of any habits, actions, or relationships that you need to let go of or change in order to live the Christian life more fully... Ask Creator God to free you...heal you...deliver you... Decide on one thing you will do to practice self-denial in order to grow healthier, to become holier.

7. Imagine that you are going to die tomorrow... Record on tape or in writing a message to your loved ones. Share this message with them, if possible.

Doris Klein

In Pursuit
of the
Vision

12.

Elizabeth Bayley Seton
Companion on Life's Journey

Elizabeth Bayley Seton was the first native-born United States saint. One of four children, the second daughter of Richard Bayley and Catherine Charlton Bayley, Elizabeth was born on August 28, 1774. The Bayleys were an Episcopalian family from New York City.

Elizabeth's mother died in childbirth when Elizabeth was three years old. In 1778 her father married Charlotte Amelia Barclay, and they had six children. Her father, a prominent physician, spent a lot of time away from home. Although Elizabeth's stepmother was attentive to Elizabeth, she focused her energy on her own children. In later years Elizabeth recalled that Charlotte introduced her to her favorite psalm—the Twenty-third Psalm.

When Elizabeth was eight years old she was sent to live with her father's relatives in a lovely rural area in New Rochelle, New York. For eight years, Elizabeth spent some of her time in New York City, where she attended school, and some of her time in the country.

Although she loved nature and experienced God's presence in Earth's splendors, Elizabeth's childhood seemed melancholic and sad. When her father went to England, Elizabeth missed him. In her diary she recalled her loneliness in his absence and the comfort she found in creation and God's loving care for her: "The air still, a clear-blue vault above, the numberless sounds of the spring melody and joy, the sweet clovers and wild flowers I had got by the way.... Still I can feel every sensation that passed through my soul.... I thought at that time my Father did not care for me. Well God was my Father, my all. I prayed—sung hymns—cried (sic)—laughed in talking to myself of how far He could place me above all sorrow then laid (sic) still to enjoy the Heavenly Peace that came over my soul."[1]

At the age of nineteen, Elizabeth married William Magee Seton on January 25, 1794. Their union was a happy one, producing six children. During the first four years of the marriage, the family business did well, but by 1800 they lost their home and the firm declared bankruptcy. When William contracted tuberculosis, he and Elizabeth, along with their oldest child, Anna Maria, sailed to Leghorn, Italy, in an attempt overcome the disease. Their plans to visit the Filicchis, who had been supportive of William's business ventures, were interrupted, however, upon their arrival. They were quarantined and confined to the ship for a month, during which time William's health deteriorated. Shortly after their release, William died and Elizabeth buried him within forty-eight hours, as required by local law.

Shocked and sorrowful, Elizabeth poured out her grief over her loss, repeating over and over this prayer: "My God, you are my God—and so I am alone in the world with you and my little ones but you are my Father and double theirs."[2] During this time of grief, the Felicci's were Elizabeth's comfort, and she came to admire their Catholic faith.

After Elizabeth returned to New York in June 1804, she expressed a growing interest in Catholicism. The correspondence between Elizabeth and her close friends reveals the influence Elizabeth's friends had on her spiritual growth. Antonio was present on March 14, 1805, when Elizabeth made her profession of faith at Saint Peter's Roman Catholic Church on Barclay Street, the only Catholic church in New York City. Elizabeth expressed her gratitude to Antonio for his support of her faith journey: "You have led me," she wrote him "to a happiness which admits of no description, and daily even hourly increases my soul's peace"[3]

Upon her embrace of Catholicism, Elizabeth experienced opposition from her friends, and the boarding house she had been operating failed. She tried to support herself by teaching, but parents withdrew their children from her school because they feared the impact she could have on their Protestant children's religious upbringing. As a result, her financial situation worsened.

One Sunday morning after Mass, in 1806, Elizabeth met William Valentine DuBourg, the president of Saint Mary's College in Baltimore. She explained to him her concern that her sons would not receive the education they needed and her desire to continue her teaching ministry. After returning to Baltimore, DuBourg discussed a number of possible solutions with Bishop John Carroll, the first United States bishop. Shortly afterwards, the two invited Elizabeth to open a school in Baltimore; Elizabeth accepted. Her sons would be able to attend Georgetown.

On June 9, 1808, Elizabeth, with her daughters, Anna, Rebecca, and Kit, moved into a small house on Paca Street in Baltimore. In the fall of that year, she opened her school with seven students: four boarders and her own three daughters. At this time her sons returned from Georgetown and studied at Saint Mary's in Baltimore.[4]

Describing a typical day in the Paca Street school, Elizabeth wrote: "In the chapel at six until eight, school at nine, dine at one, school at three, chapel at six-thirty, examination of conscience and Rosary...and so it goes without variation."[5] The school curriculum consisted of reading, arithmetic, writing, English, French, and needlework. When the number of her boarders increased, Elizabeth moved the school and her small community to Emmitsburg in the summer of 1809. By the end of July they settled in the "Stone House" and by February 1810, Elizabeth began a day school in the "White House."

In a letter to her sister-in-law, Cecilia Seton, Elizabeth shared her vision of forming a religious community: "It is expected I shall be the mother of many daughters."[6] Cecilia O'Conway, from Philadelphia, was the first woman to join Elizabeth's new community. Elizabeth professed her vows on March 25, 1809, and thereafter became known as Mother Seton. By June other young women joined her and dressed like her, in the style of a widow: black dress, leather belt, a short cape, and a white cap. Before Emmitsburg was ready, these women accompanied Elizabeth on the four-day trip, walking beside a covered wagon. The small community arrived at their destination on June 21, 1809.[7]

Life was challenging for the small community. In addition to teaching, the sisters tilled their own garden, cooked, cleaned, and did the laundry outdoors in all kinds of weather. There were only two cots in the Stone House, and these were set aside for the sick members of the community. Altogether, sixteen people lived in four rooms. Elizabeth slept on a mattress next to her daughter in the room next to the chapel. During the winter, snow often came through the roof, covering the women sleeping on the floor. Drinking water had to be hauled from an outdoor spring.[8]

As a result of these conditions, illness afflicted the community. Elizabeth's daughters, Anna and Rebecca, died of tuberculosis. Elizabeth recounted Rebecca's death: "A thousand pages could not tell the sweet hours now with my departing Rebecca…and her most tender thanksgiving that we had known and loved each other so closely here to be reunited a moment after in our dear Eternity—[It was] purest joy to see her released from the thousand pains and trials."[9]

After a long and torturous bout with tuberculosis herself, Elizabeth Seton, founder of the first American Catholic school, died peacefully on January 4, 1821, at the age of forty-six. Her community, the American Sisters of Charity, grew rapidly. In 1846, a group of Emmitsburg sisters formed a new branch in New York. Three more branches were founded in Halifax in 1856, in Convent Station in 1859, and in Cincinnati in 1852. The sisters established schools, hospitals, and orphanages—responding to human need wherever they went. Pope Paul VI canonized Elizabeth Seton on September 14, 1975.

Elizabeth Bayley Seton was a lover to her husband, a mother to her children, a soul companion to her friends, a mentor to her sisters, and an inspiration to educators throughout the world. As a parent, she nurtured her own children's growth and faced the most painful moment any parent can face—the death of her beloved children. As founder of the first Catholic school and the Sisters of Charity, Elizabeth created a religious community to respond to the divine call to share with poor children the rich treasury of Catholic beliefs and practice.

No risk was too great for Elizabeth, a pioneering spirit who trusted that God would help her overcome every obstacle. Elizabeth communicated her love and support to her friends and family through her letters. She cherished and worked at developing intimacy by sharing her love with others in a deep way. Reading her correspondences we find a powerful example of the kinship and connectedness she felt with others.

Women and men today—married couples, single parents, teachers, friends, widows, women and men in religious life—can find in Elizabeth a heart companion who truly understands the pressures and responsibilities we pilgrims encounter in our efforts to live the gospel in our world today. Not only did Elizabeth talk the talk, she walked the walk that many women today face as wives, single parents, professionals, and widows. She knew what it was like to have emotional, physical, financial, and spiritual concerns of raising and educating children alone. She knew what it was like to uproot the family, move to a new area, and start all over again without the help of friends or family.

People of all ages and lifestyles can bond with Elizabeth Seton. In a time when the material is often valued more than the spiritual, Elizabeth gives us a glimpse of the face of God. She reminds us that people who give themselves wholeheartedly to the service of others will shine as brightly as the vault of heaven, and those who lead the many to justice will shine like stars for all eternity (see Daniel 12:3). She is an exemplar of courage, faithfully persevering in the face of great difficulties. She shows us how to cope well with our setbacks and frustrations. Like Elizabeth, we can be seekers of truth, opening ourselves to the mystery of divine life—even if it means a change in the direction of our lives.

Our God is often a God of infinite surprises. Elizabeth, our sister in the faith, stands ready to befriend us on the journey. Nothing is too great or too small to share with her. In many ways she is the strong woman who has experienced so much of life's storms. In the language of today, Elizabeth went through the school of hard knocks. She relates well to contemporary women and men who struggle with problems, because she "has been there and done that." We can be assured that Elizabeth Seton will understand our greatest needs. There is no finer companion we could choose. With her inspiration, we can shine brightly with the glory in our daily lives.

Reflection

Nothing shall ever interrupt the course of my affection for you or prevent my expressing it whenever it is in my power. I am very anxious to hear of your arrival.... Do not fear to lessen my pleasure in hearing from you by so doing, for you know that one of the first rules of my happiness is to be satisfied with Good in whatever degree I can attain it; besides which it is very material that absence should not efface me from Maria's remembrance, as I have not yet lost the hope that my Anna may one day be as dear to her as you are to me. Difference of age after a certain period is very immaterial, and rather adds to affection by creating that kind of confidence we have in those who are at an age to judge of our particular feelings, and yet have more experience to give weight to advice.[10]

Discussion Starters

1. Elizabeth was a heart companion with many women. Reflect on the female power that women experience in their close relationships.

2. What message does Elizabeth Seton give, by her words and actions, about the meaning of sisterhood between women? about the meaning of friendship between women and men?

3. Have you experienced the power of friendship and/or sisterhood in your life? If so, explain.

4. How can you grow in deep intimate relationships with family members and friends?

Prayer Experience

1. Relax... Close your eyes... Concentrate on deep, slow, rhythmic breathing... With your hands placed gently on each part of your body, beginning with your feet, caress each part into relaxation... Now rest tranquilly for a few moments, enjoying the absence of tension... You are in the here and now, fully present in mind and body...

2. Be aware of the indwelling presence of Sister-God in your soul... Image yourself being held in the lap of the Sacred Feminine... Stay there as long as you can, contemplating her beauty...her power...her wisdom...her strength...her friendship...

3. Reflect on your relationship with the Feminine Divine... See yourself as an image of God... Be aware of any images, feelings, thoughts, or insights this image stirs in you...

4. Name and give thanks for those women in your life who have listened to your pain and loved you into healing...

5. Reflect on times when you experienced deep solidarity with these sisters of your soul... Recall how you felt...what you learned...how these relationships helped you grow spiritually...

6. Dialogue with Elizabeth Seton... Imagine yourself talking and sharing with her... Now go deeper into your center where your souls meet... Let separateness fall away... Let Sister-Love make you one

in heart and mind... Be aware that Divine Love, who is vividly and passionately feminine, connects you with your soul sister on a level that you can scarcely even imagine...

7. Imagine a special celebration with Elizabeth Seton... Imagine what you do...where you are...who else celebrates with you...the special sharing you enjoy with Elizabeth... Before you leave the celebration, something special happens that you'll never forget... Imagine what that is... As you conclude your prayer, open your eyes and continue inhaling deeply through your nose and exhaling through your mouth for several minutes... Be aware that as you breathe in and out, you send Sister-God's warm, tender love to your friend Elizabeth and you receive Sister-God's love through her... After the prayer experience do something special with a soul friend to celebrate Sister-God's love.

Running
from
the
Vision

13.

Elizabeth Lange

Model of Trust in Divine Providence

*E*lizabeth Lange was born of San Domingan parents—a white father and a Black mother—around 1784, in what is now Haiti. Elizabeth was considered "colored." Her father had some financial and social status in the community, and her mother was a loving, spiritual woman who spent the final days of her life in the Baltimore convent established by her daughter.

Little is known about Elizabeth's early years in San Domingo and in the United States.[1] Some records show that Elizabeth, accompanied by family members, entered the United States at Philadelphia in 1812.[2] We do know that forty years before the Civil War, Elizabeth settled in Baltimore. During this time, Baltimore had became a haven for French Catholics who were fleeing violent upheaval in San Domingo. Maryland, however, was a slave-owning colony where prejudice against people of color was prevalent and education for Blacks almost unheard of. From her early years, Elizabeth had a vision of peace in the midst of this oppression. With a small income from her father and with the help of a friend, Marie Balas, she chose to live her dream by offering free education in her home to children of color.[3]

The Sulpician priests, themselves refugees of the French Revolution, operated a parish church at Saint Mary's Seminary in Baltimore, where whites celebrated Eucharist on the upper floor while people of color worshipped in the basement. When Sulpician priest Father James Joubert became the pastor for the Black congregation, he discovered that the children in his catechism class were illiterate. As Joubert was formulating the idea of establishing a school for them, he learned that Elizabeth and a few other women in the Black congregation had already operated a free school for nearly ten years. The school, however, survived on a veritable shoestring with a constant shortage of funds. Joubert sought and received the support of Archbishop James Whitfield to establish a school for the education of children of color. Joubert, impressed by Elizabeth's dedication, asked her to be the cornerstone of his plan. His diary reports her response, "And she agreed."[4]

Before beginning to plan the school, however, Joubert invited Elizabeth to join with him in founding a community of Black women who would be dedicated to the ministry of teaching. Up to this time, no religious order permitted Blacks to join their communities. Nonetheless, Joubert requested and received initial approval from Archbishop Whitfield to establish Elizabeth Lange's religious community. On July 2, 1829, four women—Elizabeth Lange, Marie Balas, Almaide Duchemin, and Rosanne Boegue—pronounced their vows. In a small ceremony following Joubert's 6:00 a.m. Mass, surrounded by a small gathering of friends, the Oblate Sisters of Providence made history by becoming the first religious order of Black women in the United States, founded in a slave state before the Emancipation Proclamation. They wore a habit consisting of a black dress, cape, and bonnet.[5] Their rule clearly affirmed their identity and mission: "The Oblate Sisters of Providence are a Religious Society of virgins and widows of color. Their end is to consecrate themselves to God in a special manner not only to sanctify themselves and thereby secure the glory of God, but also to work for the Christian education of colored children." Elizabeth's new name became Sister Mary.[6]

Sister Mary and her companions began their work in a rented house at Number Five Saint Mary's Court, with twenty girl students:

eleven boarders and nine day students. Before the year ended, however, the landlord gave notice that they would have to move. Because of racial discrimination on the part of many landlords, the women encountered difficulty renting another property. Finally an affluent, white benefactor of San Domingan background, Doctor Chatard, offered them another house at a token rent. The occupants of the house, however, were unable to vacate immediately, so the sisters had to take temporary housing at 610 George Street.[7]

The Oblate Sisters endured verbal insults as well as threats of physical violence from some of Baltimore's white Catholics who were angered by women of color wearing a religious habit. Even members of the clergy expressed hostility. But Father Joubert continued his commitment to the small congregation and visited them almost daily. Finally, on October 2, 1831, Pope Gregory XVI officially recognized the Oblate Sisters of Providence as a religious community. They didn't received this wonderful news, however, until five months later, in March 1832.[8]

When Father Joubert informed the archbishop of the discrimination that the oblates were encountering, the archbishop promised to defend the fledgling order: "Monsieur Joubert, it is not lightly, but with reflection that I approved your project. I knew and saw the finger of God. Besides, have I not the power to make foundations in my diocese, in my episcopal city, of any religious establishment whatever?" Elizabeth later praised Joubert as the closest friend that the oblates ever had.[9]

There is little information about Elizabeth Lange, or Sister Mary, in the official records of the community. She evidently spoke fluent Spanish and French and knew only rudimentary English—enough to be able to communicate with her community. She was described as petite, powerful, and physically and spiritually strong: "Sister Mary never spared herself. She seldom rested. If there was work to be done, she was the first to volunteer."[10]

In 1832 a cholera epidemic broke out in Baltimore, New York, and Philadelphia, and Elizabeth and four oblates devoted themselves to caring for the sick around the clock. When trustees of the Baltimore Bureau of the Poor asked if some of the religious communities would be able to care for people in the almshouse hospital, eleven oblates volunteered and four Sisters of Charity served. Although the Baltimore City Council later published a public thanks to the Sisters of Charity, there was no public acknowledgment of the oblate sisters. The archbishop and his housekeeper had been nursed back to health by an Oblate Sister, Sister Anthony, who later died of the illness. She was buried in the cathedral cemetery — in the colored section.[11]

The oblate school fostered a warm, homelike atmosphere, with teachers and students sharing the same rooms and activities. The sisters and children had recreation together in the morning, and the rosary was recited at noon. Mother Lange usually read a few verses from the Bible, in French, after which all shared the afternoon meal. At 5:00 p.m., after spiritual reading, the sisters and children sewed or knitted together until the evening meal. After supper, all participated in recreation until the bell rang for silence. Prayers were said at 8:30, and sisters and students retired. It was only then that, along with their other duties, the sisters made vestments as another source of income for the community.[12]

After Father Joubert and Archbishop Whitfield died in 1844, the new archbishop, Samuel Eccleston, reasserted the belief that the education of Black children was useless and a low priority. He expressed hope that the oblate order would be disbanded. When support for the oblates education ministry was requested, Eccleston allegedly retorted, "What good is it?" Some of the Baltimore clergy suggested that for Black women, being competent servants was more important than being nuns.[13]

Even more discouraging was the fact that ecclesiastical authorities would not provide for the spiritual needs of the sisters, leaving the oblates without a regular chaplain and the celebration of Mass. They had no support from the bishop or from most of the pastors of the city. "They stood in front of St. Alphonsus Church hoping for spiritual comfort from some busy Redemptorist who might speak French. They were cold, hungry, and discouraged, since even the ecclesiastical authorities suggested the dissolution of the community and the Sisters' return to the world."[14]

Marie Balas, one of the original foundresses, died in 1845. By that time, the school enrollment had dropped to twenty children, ten of whom were orphans. There were only fourteen professed sisters, the community had a debt of $700, and two of the founding sisters supported the community by working in the seminary kitchen. The other sisters took in laundry to feed themselves and the children in their care.[15]

By September 1847 the oblates were down to twelve members, and Archbishop Eccleston advised them to disband and return to the world. When Father Anwander, a young Redemptorist, learned of the oblates' plight, he informed his superior, Father John Neumann. Neumann advised Anwander to ask permission to become the oblates' spiritual director. Following his superior's directive, Anwander met with the archbishop and, dropping to his knees, begged, "Most Reverend Father, only give me your blessing, with your permission, on trial." Archbishop Eccleston agreed, and the young Redemptorist was able to begin that very day to minister to the sisters' needs.[16]

Because Anwander canvassed the city of Baltimore trying to recruit tuition-paying students from the Black communities, both donations and enrollment increased. The oblates doubled their numbers, and the school attracted one hundred day students and sixty boarders. Another school soon was built that enrolled between fifty to sixty boys. With this rebirth, Archbishop Eccleston and the clergy of the city became more supportive, and the Catholic people of color of Baltimore were formed into their own congregation, with a church on Calvert Street.[17]

When the Civil War began in 1860, Father Anwander was reassigned, after thirteen years with the oblates, and the direction of the order was given over to the Jesuits. Father Miller, their new chaplain, helped the sisters through the difficult war years, when racial bigotry and hatred were common experiences. In 1866 the Jesuits bought a house adjacent to their own residence, with the agreement that in exchange for use of the house, the sisters would do the washing and mending for nearby Loyola College.

In 1866 the bishops at the Second Plenary Council of Baltimore pleaded for more priests to dedicate themselves to "the service of colored people."[18] Meanwhile, the Oblate Sisters tried to open schools in other states, but they encountered a lack of diocesan support, Black parents too impoverished to pay tuition, and white Catholics unwilling to contribute. The new schools that the oblates started in New Orleans, Philadelphia, and Fells Point, Maryland had to close for the same reason: lack of funds.[19]

When Father Miller's health failed, the Josephite Order, whose members were already working in Baltimore's first Black parish, was assigned to provide pastoral care for the oblates.[20] Before she died, Elizabeth finally received the public support from civic and Church leaders that she had hoped for all her life. At the order's golden jubilee celebration on July 2, 1879, many representatives from civic and ecclesiastical organizations expressed respect and gratitude to the oblates for their work in the community. The oblate annals describe Elizabeth's response: "[Mother Mary] received everyone and everything with thanks and respect." Three years later, in the presence of her dear friend, Father Anwander, and loving oblates, Elizabeth died peacefully on February 3, 1882.[21]

Elizabeth Lange is a heroic role model for African-American Catholics. She was an educator of faith and vision who, through the foundation of her community, saved Black American Catholics from "the destructive forces of a society which tried to keep them illiterate."[22] Bishop Carl Fisher refers to her as "a modern example for all people who seek to place their trust in God even in the midst of adversity.... A woman who faced tremendous opposition, discouragement and defections among her closest followers, yet, never lost faith in God."[23]

Elizabeth Lange belongs to all of us. She shows us how to persevere in following our dreams, regardless of the obstacles or opposition. She demonstrates a love that survives crisis, difficulty, prejudice, hatred, and poverty. As a champion of God's justice and peace for refugees and people of color, she calls us to struggle against ignorance, injustice, and discrimination in our world today. As a change agent who gave birth to the first religious order of Black women in the United States, Elizabeth challenges us to be initiators of new ideas, fresh approaches, and creative programs that bring forth life, healing, and hope for all God's people. She walks with us as a companion on the long journey to freedom, equality, and love, encouraging us to trust always in Divine Providence.

Reflection

Mother Mary Elizabeth Lange and her early daughters were refugees. This community, always poor, almost coming to an end once, persevering, taking on new life, was supported always by the Foundresses' abiding confidence in God. Mother Mary Lange began her work, [and it] increased in numbers without resources. When authorities of the Church abandoned her, God, in unexpected ways, raised up champions for her cause. She lived through terrible disappointments and rose above hard opposition. As difficulties mounted, her hope grew. Even when her ideals failed to triumph, she would not accept defeat. Mother Lange's life was filled with frustration. Frustration in the sense that her service, the reality of her vision, was always restricted by forces she could in no way control. Living with and rising above such frustration calls for fortitude. And Mary Lange's fortitude came from her faith that the things she believed in, her dream, and the things she tried to do, her reality of service, were right and just and good.

Mother Mary Elizabeth Lange's story [*The Story of the Oblate Sisters of Providence*] has a place in the annals of religious orders, in the history of the Catholic Church in the United States, in the secular history of the United States. Her daughters share a legacy of courage, hope, and vision unsurpassed in modern times.[24]

Discussion Starters

1. When authorities of the Catholic Church abandoned Elizabeth Lange, God raised up champions for her cause. How has the Church discriminated against Blacks in the past? How is the Church an advocate for racial justice and harmony today? What more can the Church

do, by education and example, to become a leader in issues such as affirmative action?

2. Elizabeth Lange lived through terrible disappointments and rose above hard opposition. What can we learn from Elizabeth about trust in Divine Providence?

3. Elizabeth and the Oblate Sisters of Providence encountered racial bigotry. Have you ever experienced discrimination based on race, gender, national origin, age, or disability? If so, how did you respond? If not, how would you respond if it happened to you today?

4. Elizabeth Lange is a role model not only for African-American Catholics, but for all people. She shows us how to persevere against ignorance, racism, and injustice. What does Elizabeth Lange's story tell us about courage, vision, and hope?

Prayer Experience

1. Look at a spot on the ceiling or up at the sky. Stare at the spot without moving any muscles, and take several deep breaths, exhaling deeply each time... Now close your eyes... As each muscle and nerve becomes limp, let go of all your tensions and concerns... From head to toe, feel calm and serene... Relax deeper and deeper with each breath you take... Be aware that you are in the embrace of Divine Providence... You are being loved fully...loved completely...loved totally... You feel at home... You feel safe... You feel open... Take a deep breath and exhale... When you are ready, open your eyes.

2. Reread Elizabeth Lange's story and the Reflection in a quiet and leisurely manner...

3. Dialogue with Elizabeth about her trust in Divine Providence... Imagine the disappointment she suffered... Imagine the racial bigotry she suffered... Imagine the injustice she suffered... Share with Elizabeth similar struggles you have had in your life... Be present together in Divine Providence...

4. Be aware of how Divine Providence has been present in your life in the midst of adversity...in times of disappointment...in the face of oppositionv... Offer thanks for each occasion that comes to mind...

5. Imagine Divine Providence revealing to you some new dreams... remarkable visions...great ideas...deep insights...exciting plans... challenging programs...promising projects...satisfying relation-ships... Take time to explore Divine Providence...to enjoy Divine Providence...to be energized by Divine Providence... Compose a prayer, song, dance, poem, or psalm to celebrate Divine Providence.

6. Ask Divine Providence to help you grow in faith, trust, and courage... Decide on one practical way you can foster racial justice and harmony in your community, in your neighborhood, in the world.

7. Celebrate your experience of Divine Providence in some special way. As you do so, be conscious of any images, thoughts, feelings, insights, or sensations that emerge. You may wish to record these in your prayer journal or express them in poetry, song, dance, art, or some other way.

Empowered
with the
Vision

Doris Klein CSA

14.

Sojourner Truth

Woman of Courage

Sojourner Truth, as her "freed" name was later to become, was born into slavery in Swartekill, in Ulster County, New York, around 1797. She was given the "slave" name, Isabella. Her parents, Betsey and James, were of African ancestry and were owned, as she was, by the Hardenberghs, a wealthy Dutch family.[1] Consequently, the only language that Isabella and her parents spoke was Dutch.

Johannes Hardenbergh had been a member of the New York, colonial assembly and an officer in the Revolutionary War. A landowner and owner of a grist mill, he held seven slaves. After Johannes Hardenbergh died, Isabella and her parents became the property of his son, Charles, who lived in the Swartekill area. Charles housed his slaves in a dark, dirty, damp, one-room cellar where, according to Isabella's recollection, everyone slept on straw laid on loose floor boards.

It was in this setting that Isabella's mother was to give birth to ten or twelve children, Isabella being the second youngest. Most of these children had been sold before Isabella could remember. She would remember, however, how her parents would spend hours talking about their children "recounting every endearing, as well as harrowing circumstance that taxed memory could supply, from the histories of those dear departed ones, of whom they had been robbed."[2]

Charles Hardenbergh died when Isabella was around nine years old. After his death, the Hardenbergh family decided to free James and Betsey; James was too old to work, and Betsey needed her freedom to care for him. Isabella and her brother, however, were sold separately. From that point on, Isabella rarely saw her parents. She did find out later that her mother died first and her father, blind and infirmed, was abandoned by the Hardenberghs to survive however he could in a small shanty in the woods. One winter, according to a story Isabella told, an aged, sick, Black woman named Soan came upon James in his shanty. He begged Soan to stay and care for him, but Soan herself was old, timid, and weak, with no one to care for her. She reluctantly concluded that she must leave him. Soon after this visit, James died—sick, blind, frozen, and alone.[3]

Isabella recalled that she was sold for one hundred dollars to John Neely, an owner of a store in Kingston on Rondout Creek. The Neelys spoke only English and Isabella still spoke only Dutch. When Isabella did not understand an order that she was given, she was severely beaten. She described one such horrific scene: "When he had tied her hands together before her, he gave her the most cruel whipping she was ever tortured with. He whipped her till the flesh was deeply lacerated, and the blood streamed from her wounds—and the scars remain to the present day, to testify to the fact."[4]

After a year or two with the Neelys, Isabella again was sold, this time to Martinus Schryver, a tavern owner and fisherman who lived in Kingston. Isabella did outdoor work and ran errands for Schryver, and was treated better, even given more freedom to come and go. Sometimes when she was outside, she would look at the white-sailed sloops on the Hudson and occasionally observe among them the new steamboats shooting black smoke into the air.[5]

In 1810 Isabella was sold to John Dumont, who owned a farm in West Park along the Hudson River. Dumont affirmed Isabella for her abilities to do heavy farm work. In turn, she worked harder. During this time, Robert, a slave from a neighboring farm, began to visit

Isabella, even though his master, Charles Catton, had forbidden him to do so. One Saturday afternoon, when Robert came to visit, Catton and his son followed him. Isabella looked out from her upstairs window as the Cattons "fell upon him like tigers, beating him with the heavy ends of their canes, bruising and mangling his head and face in the most awful manner, and causing the blood, which streamed from his wounds, to cover him like a slaughtered beast." Dumont, witnessing this attack, intervened, saying that he did not want "no niggers killed here." The Cattons then tied Robert's hands behind him and led him away. As a result of this viscous beating, Robert no longer came to visit Isabella. Instead, he married a woman from among the Catton's slaves and did not live many years afterwards.[6]

Isabella eventually married Tom, another slave on the Dumont farm. According to her *Narrative,* Isabella and Tom were married "after the fashion of slavery, one of the slaves performing the ceremony for them." After some time, Isabella "found herself the mother of five children and she rejoiced in being permitted to be the instrument of increasing the property of her oppressors!"[7] Her children were named Diana, Peter, Elizabeth, and Sophia; the fifth child did not live long. Isabella's *Narrative* does not indicate who the father was of each of her children, but the assumption is that Tom fathered them all. Some historians, however, think that Robert was the father of Isabella's first child.[8]

Dumont promised that he would free Isabella and Tom on July 4, 1826, and give them a log cabin for a home. This was a year earlier than slaves were to be freed in the State of New York. Dumont failed to keep his promise, however, and in the fall of 1826, Isabella plotted to escape from the Dumont farm.

One morning just before daybreak, carrying her infant Sophia in her arms, Isabella simply walked away. She explained what her mindset had been at that time: "I thought it was mean to run away, but I could walk away." She left the other children in the care of her husband, Tom, who chose to stay at the Dumont's.[9]

The Van Wagenens, who disapproved of slavery and had known Isabella since she was a child, gave her shelter. When Dumont appeared to take Isabella back into slavery and she refused to go with him, Isaac Van Wagenen intervened and offered Dumont twenty-five dollars to give up his claim on Isabella's services. The two men agreed, and Isabella was free at last.[10]

When Isabella learned that Dumont had sold her son, Peter, to a man who then sent the boy to work on a plantation in Alabama, she pleaded with the Dumonts and the new owners to bring him back, but her appeals were to no avail. Fortunately some of the Van Wagenens' friends informed Isabella that there was a law against sending slaves out of the state, and that she could sue to get her son back. So Isabella went from door to door asking for donations so that she could hire a lawyer. She collected enough money, and the lawyer arranged to have Peter brought to New York for a court hearing. At the hearing, Peter protested that Isabella was not his mother and pleaded with his master not to force him to go with her. The judge, suspecting that the slave master had threatened Peter—which proved to be the case—released the boy to Isabella. At that time, it was unprecedented for a Black woman to win a court case against a white man.[11]

In 1828 Isabella moved to New York City and found decent work as a domestic servant in the homes of wealthy families. There she joined a group of evangelists who walked through the streets singing hymns to the poor. She devoted her free time to teaching young homeless women how to cook, sew, and clean houses, so that they could find work as household servants.

By 1843 Isabella grew tired of this work and the city. She spent a summer on Long Island, preaching to potato farmers and ministering to the sick in exchange for shelter and food. Here she fully realized the reality of her freedom, and that charity was to be her calling. To celebrate this awakening, she changed her name to Sojourner Truth. Eventually she traveled to Massachusetts, the center of the abolitionist movement, and joined the Northampton Association of Education and Industry. There she became involved in the anti-slavery movement and met prominent public leaders and abolitionists, such as William Lloyd Garrison and Frederick Douglas.

In 1846 Truth went to work in the home of one of the abolitionist organizers, George Benson. Shortly afterwards, a friend, Olive Gilbert, volunteered to write Truth's memoirs. Gilbert thought that

Truth's account of her life as a slave would help turn the tide against slavery in the North.

Thus *The Narrative of Sojourner Truth: A Northern Slave* was published in 1850. Fearing anti-slavery backlash, however, no book-store would sell the work. So Truth herself took copies of her book to public meetings, where she succeeded in selling hundreds of them.[12]

In addition to the anti-slavery movement, Truth joined the women's rights movement, where she met some of the most outspoken women of her time: Lucretia Mott, Amy Post, and Elizabeth Cady Stanton. These women raised money for the abolitionists, taught former slaves to read, organized anti-slavery meetings, printed anti-slavery pamphlets, and helped slaves escape by the Underground Railroad, a network of safe houses for escaped slaves on the difficult and dangerous journey to Canada, where they would be free. In 1848 Elizabeth Cady Stanton and Lucretia Mott organized the first con-vention for women's rights in Seneca Falls, New York. The Seneca Falls Declaration of Rights and Sentiments demanded that women be given the right to vote and be treated as full citizens. At a women's rights convention in Worcester, Massachusetts, in 1850, Sojourner Truth, after listening to the other speakers talk about equal pay for equal work, declared: "Sisters, I'm not clear what you be after. If women want any rights more than they've got, why don't they just take them and not be talking about it."[13]

Opponents sometimes confronted Truth and argued that women, according to the Christian message, should be silent and learn from their husbands. In defense of women, Truth argued that Jesus "never used a harsh word in speaking to them, but called men 'a generation of vipers.' As for the assumed superiority of men because Jesus was male, Truth asked men, 'How came Jesus into the world?' Through God who created him and woman who bore him. Man, where is your part?'"[14]

Advocating women's right to vote was only one of the issues of the women's rights movement in the 1850s. Women also asked for equal rights at home, at school, and at work. If women could vote, Truth believed, they could hold positions in which they could advo-cate women's interests, such as women in Congress, women judges, women lawyers, and women on juries. She argued that women in government would bring reform. "As men have been endeavoring for years to govern alone," she argued, "and have not yet succeeded in perfecting any system, it is about time the women should take the matter in hand." She likewise thought women would bring peace to the country. "I want to see women have their rights, and then there will be no more war...but when we have women's rights, there is nothing to fight for...All the battles that have ever been was for self-ishness."[15]

Sojourner Truth spent most of the second half of her life speaking out against slavery and campaigning for women's rights. Her travels took her to more than twenty states throughout the Midwest and New England. In 1870, when she was about seventy-three years old, Truth pleaded with President Grant and Congress to give some western land to the freed slaves. Even though Congress applauded her speech, they failed to act. Eventually, however, freed slaves moved West to begin new lives anyway. Truth traveled to Kansas to see her dream come true. Her people, former slaves, were reading, writing, and working their own land. "Thank you, Lord," she whispered, "You've given me a new song."[16]

Truth spent her last years with her family at her home near Battle Creek, Michigan, and her children and grandchildren were present when she died. "Don't fret, child," she said to one of her children in her dying moments. "I'm going home like a shooting star." She died on November 26, 1883, and was buried in her dark dress, with a white scarf around her neck and a white turban over her hair.[17]

As a champion of Black emancipation and women's rights, Sojourner Truth was a courageous woman whose voice helped free many people from slavery and injustice. Her journey to freedom has been a source of inspiration to women and men throughout the world who continue the struggle for civil rights and justice for all people. Truth stirred up consciousness, among white, upper and middle-class feminists, that womanhood included Black women, poor women, uneducated women—all women.

Sojourner Truth's powerful words and strong witness continue to challenge women today to foster solidarity with oppressed women throughout the world. Women have much to share and learn from one another—especially from women of color, uneducated women, poor women, and women from other cultures and lands. When women of the world unite, what a mighty power for justice and love the human family will experience.

Reflection

"That man over there," she said, looking at the minister who claimed that a woman's place was to be a wife, mother, companion, sister, and niece. Among other things he also said women were the "weaker sex"...

[Sojourner challenged this view of women's roles.] "He says women need to be helped into carriages and lifted over ditches and to have the best everywhere. Nobody ever helps me into carriages, over mud puddles, or gets me any best places."

...And raising herself to her full height, she asked, "And ain't I a woman?"...

[Sojourner turned around to the men who were seated behind her.] "Look at me!" She bared her right arm and raised it in the air. The audience gasped as one voice. Her dark arm was muscular, made strong by hard work. "I have ploughed. And I have planted. And I have gathered into barns. And no man could head me." Pausing, briefly, she whispered, "And ain't I a woman?"...

"I have borne [13] children and seen them sold into slavery, and when I cried out in a mother's grief, none heard me but Jesus. And ain't I a woman?"... [Sojourner had five children. She was probably referring to her mother here.]

[Then she challenged her male religious critics.] "You say Jesus was a man so that means God favors men over women. Where did your Christ come from?" She asked again, "Where did he come from?" Then she answered her own question, "From God and a woman. Man had nothing to do with him"...

[She disputed the popular perception that women were less intelligent than men.] "Suppose a man's mind holds a quart, and woman's don't hold but a pint; if her pint is full, it's as good as a quart...

"If the first woman God ever made was strong enough to turn the world upside down all alone, these women together ought to be able to turn it back and get it right-side up again and now that they are asking to do it, the men better let 'em."[18]

Discussion Starters

1. How is Sojourner Truth a role model for us today?

2. Sojourner Truth spoke out against racial and gender discrimination. What is the connection between these two forms of oppression? Why is it important to make this connection?

3. How was religion used to justify the enslavement of Blacks and women? How can religion be used to liberate all people from every type of oppression?

4. How have brain studies been used to discriminate against Blacks and women in education and jobs? What can be done to turn this around? Have affirmative action programs been successful in obtaining equality for minorities and women in the workplace? Why?

Prayer Experience

1. Be aware of any tension in your body... Release the tension by breathing relaxation into this area of your body... As you inhale, breathe in the Spirit's freeing power... As you exhale, allow the liberating presence of the Holy One to flow out of you and fill the world with healing...

2. Imagine Sojourner Truth's early life as a slave... Imagine the deprivations...the beatings...the hard work...the deplorable living conditions...the separation from family... Be aware of persons and institutions in the past that supported slavery...that supported prejudice...that supported discrimination... Be aware of persons and institutions today that advocate discrimination in more subtle ways... Open yourself to the Spirit of freedom... Invite this Spirit to guide you... Decide on an appropriate response or action that you will take to oppose prejudice and live in peace with people of different races, genders, color, and national origin.

3. Imagine Sojourner Truth preaching and speaking out for Black emancipation and women's rights... Meditate on her "Ain't I a Woman?" speech... Become aware of ways poor women, uneducated women, and women of color "preach" today by their words and example, which are powerful sermons on the Spirit's love... Name, affirm, and give thanks for these women...

4. Imagine that you have been invited to preach a sermon or give a speech on race and/or gender equality. Listen to the Spirit speak deeply within you... Reflect on your own experiences and the experiences of others... Now imagine yourself speaking out with vigor, humility, and courage... Be aware of any feelings, insights, thoughts, and images that emerge ...

5. Share your thoughts, feelings, insights, and images with the Spirit in a prayerful dialogue... If you would like, write the conversation you have with the Holy One about race/gender equality.

6. Read what you have written in this dialogue. Now be aware of the Spirit's liberating power bringing you, others, the Church, society, and the world out of the darkness of prejudice into the light of freedom...

7. Light a candle and reflect on God's freeing love as the light shining in the darkness of discrimination... Be aware of any areas of darkness...any inner blockages...any areas in which you, others, the Church, and society need to experience liberation from the blindness of bigotry and bias... Contemplate divine love transforming each area of darkness... Experience the purifying power of light filling everyone... Imagine all people discovering their profound union with one another... Imagine that all rejoice as one in divine love... Imagine all living in peace, harmony, and justice—respectful of one another and of Earth... Do something to celebrate your connectedness with people of different races, genders, creeds, and national origins.

Is this
Really the
Vision?

Doris Klein

15.

Frances Xavier Cabrini

Advocate of the Powerless

rances Cabrini was born and baptized on July 15, 1850, in
Lombardy, Italy, the youngest of thirteen children of
Agostino and Stella Cabrini. As a child, Frances loved to
pray and when she was eleven years old, she took a private vow of
chastity.

At the time of her confirmation, Frances had a powerful spiritual
experience. "The moment I was anointed with the sacred chrism I felt
what I shall never be able to express…I seemed no longer on earth.
My heart was replete with a most pure joy…." Unable to explain her
experience, Frances only knew that it was the Holy Spirit.[1]

Rosa, her sister, took charge of Frances's upbringing. As the village
schoolmistress, she guided Frances's education until Frances was thirteen years old. After that Frances attended Daughters of the Sacred
Heart School in Arluno where, at eighteen, she obtained her teaching
license. After graduation, she wanted to enter the Daughters of the
Sacred Heart, but they would not accept her because of her frail health.

At this time Don Antonio Serrati convinced Frances to begin
charitable work at the House of Providence orphanage in Codogno.
There Frances and seven other women made their vows in September

1877. They worked hard to support this institution but in 1880 the bishop of Lodi, Domenico Gelmini, closed it. When Frances met with him on November 12, he advised her: "You want to be a missionary Sister. The time is ripe. I do not know any institute of missionary Sisters, so found one yourself." She replied: "I will look for a house."[2]

After the bishop closed the orphanage, Frances and her seven companions moved into an empty house on November 10, 1880. Frances was appointed prioress of this community, which would later be known as the Institute of Missionary Sisters of the Sacred Heart. Hoping that this new foundation would become a worldwide missionary order, Frances Cabrini reminded Bishop Gelmini, "Don't think that my Institute can be confined to one city or one diocese. The whole world is not wide enough for me."[3] Between 1882 and 1887 Frances opened seven houses in northern Italy and a free school and nursery in Rome. On March 12, 1888, the institute received formal approval from Rome.

Even though Frances had hoped to be a missionary in China, she was persuaded by Leo XIII and Bishop Giovanni Battista Scalabrini of Piacenza to work among Italian immigrants in the United States. Archbishop Corrigan wrote from New York, promising a house to the sisters. So on March 23, 1889, Frances sailed to New York with six companions. On their arrival, they were met by two priests who had no accommodations ready for them. As a result, the sisters spent their first night in New York in a filthy rooming house crawling with so many bedbugs and rodents that they could not even lie down. When they called on Archbishop Corrigan the next day, they learned that there was, in fact, no convent for them, and they were encouraged to return to Italy. But Frances refused to go home. "No, your Excellency," she said, shaking her head deliberately. "No. We cannot do that. I came to New York under obedience to the Holy Father. Here I shall remain." The archbishop looked at her: "He could see that the diminutive nun before him was not intending the slightest disrespect, and he admired her courage."[4] When he asked Frances if she had any proof that the pope had sent her, Frances gave him several letters demonstrating ecclesiastical authorization. One letter, signed by

Cardinal Simeoni, the Prefect of Proganganda, stated that Frances Cabrini had come "by order of this Sacred Congregation," which indicated "by order of the pope." At that point, Corrigan was impressed by Frances's candor and determination, and knew that he would have to relent and allow her to remain.[5]

An American named Mary Reid, married to an Italian count, assisted the new arrivals. She rented a house for the sisters at 43 East 59th Street. The archbishop initially refused to allow Frances to take possession of the house because he feared that the presence of Italian children in this fashionable neighborhood would arouse the growing American antagonism against foreigners. After Frances and Mary met with the archbishop to discuss his reservations, however, he realized that arguing with the women was futile and gave permission for them to move into the house. In four months they had gathered four hundred destitute children at this orphanage.[6]

Frances soon realized that the archbishop had been justified in his concern for the location of the convent. Political leaders threatened her and her community with legal restrictions. In her imagination, Frances had envisaged a large country estate with a farm-like atmosphere and acres of woods, large gardens, and lots of birds, chickens, goats, and cows. She wanted only the best environment for the orphans.

When Frances shared her dream with Corrigan, he suggested that they take a carriage ride along the Hudson River. When they arrived at Peekskill, Frances pointed to the opposite shore, to a cluster of lovely buildings situated on top of a hill. "Ah, Excellence," she cried out with delight, "there, that is the place where our orphans should be!" The archbishop replied, "Mother Cabrini, that is a large estate belonging to the Jesuits. Shall I look into the matter? Could it be…is it possible Our Lord wants them to sell?" She shook her head, "It may be Our Lord's wish…and He may be waiting for Your Excellence to suggest His wish to the Jesuits—and at a bargain of course!"[7] As it turned out, the Jesuits were willing to sell the estate at a much lower price than they paid for it because the well had gone dry and they had not been able to locate water. When they expressed their concern about this, Frances smiled and addressed their doubts: "Dear

Brothers, remove that concern from your conscience and let it rest upon my shoulders. If our Lord wants me to raise…children here in West Park, He will have to bring water."[8] She prayed to Our Lady of Graces for help in finding water and, sure enough, in a dream, Mary appeared to Frances instructing her where to dig the well. Frances followed the directions exactly and discovered a beautiful mountain spring with clear, crystal water. At that spot Frances placed a statue of the Blessed Mother.[9]

In New York Frances founded schools, orphanages, religious education classes, and Columbia Hospital. During the years that followed, her reputation became widespread, and she received requests to found schools and orphanages in different parts of the globe. This energetic woman and her sisters crossed the ocean thirty times within thirty-five years to establish hospitals, schools, orphanages, and convents throughout Europe and in Central and South America, as well as the United States. The whole world was the field of operations for the Missionary Sisters.

Frances had an adventurous spirit and insisted on being present during the start-up days of her foundations in different countries. On one such occasion, when she was traveling by mule across the Andes Mountains, Mother Cabrini had to dismount and jump across a chasm. Unfortunately she didn't quite clear the chasm. Mercifully her muleteer caught her, saving her from falling hundreds of feet down a steep precipice.

Undaunted by this near mishap, Mother Cabrini continued the daring journey through the falling snow to Buenos Aires. There she met with the archbishop who agreed to support a house of the Missionary Sisters, thus spurring her to select a building in the town center for her new school. The Argentineans, so impressed and enthusiastic about this new facility, sent their children in large numbers.[10]

Frances Cabrini died of malaria in Columbus Hospital in Chicago on December 22, 1917. At the time of her death, there were more than fifteen hundred Missionary Sisters of the Sacred Heart and sixty-seven convents throughout the world. At her canonization on July 7, 1946, Pope Pius XII said, "Although her constitution was very frail, her spirit was endowed with such singular strength that, knowing the will of God in her regard, she permitted nothing to impede her from accomplishing what seemed beyond the strength of a woman."[11] Since she had become a naturalized citizen in 1909, Frances Cabrini became the first American saint.

People today marvel at Frances Cabrini's savvy, business sense, and energetic, activist spirit. She had a passionate vision of a world-wide missionary institute, and simply believed that the people, money, and resources would appear when she needed them—and they did. She was able to collect small sums of money from Italian immigrants, but from wealthy people, whom she seemed to select at random, she was able to obtain large donations. One incident demonstrates her enterprising style. After a Mr. Wentworth refused to see her, she waited around the corner from his office until he finally appeared. When she cornered him, he expressed his irritation: "What is it you have got to sell?" "Sell, Mr. Wentworth? Sell? Only children." He looked at her with disbelief as she continued her message: "When you began as a businessman, Mr. Wentworth, you had dreams. You must have had dreams to have been successful in business. Well, I have dreams too. Different dreams from yours, perhaps, but still dreams." She received a generous donation from him that day—as she often did using that very same tactic.[12]

During her lifetime and after, Frances Cabrini performed many miracles. For example, a sister was cured of varicose veins when she put on a pair of Frances's white cotton stockings.[13] Another sister, Delfino Grazioli, was cured of adhesions of the pylorus and duodenum which, according to doctors, was an incurable condition. When one of the nurses accidentally blinded a newborn baby by washing his eyes with fifty-percent solution of nitrate of silver, the child's sight was restored when his eyes were touched with a relic of Mother Cabrini.[14]

Today more than ever, we need the faith, strength, and stamina of Mother Cabrini. Like her, we need to see the obstacles and problems of life as opportunities to grow strong in our Christian faith. We need her vision to dream new dreams, and her courage to make these dreams happen so that the powerless can be empowered. In sum, all of us can be missionaries. All of us can be involved in helping others have a better life. All we need are hearts fired with God's love for all people, especially children who are poor, abandoned, abused, addicted, and neglected.

Let us, like Saint Frances Cabrini, do something concrete to care for the people in our area who have little or nothing. Perhaps we can start by tutoring a child, teaching English to new arrivals in our country, or helping an unemployed person find a decent-paying job. Then, like Mother Cabrini, we will be change agents helping to solve society's problems—one person at a time.

Reflection

After Frances Cabrini acquired the Jesuit property on the Hudson River, one of her sisters asked: "Mother, did you get the beautiful land and houses?"

"Of course, my daughters. I had made up my mind to do so even before I got there."

"Forgive me, Mother, but where is the money to put down? We have not a cent in the bank."

"The Jesuits are packing and going to another monastery they have built in Peekskill. I told them Our Lord is my banker and will not fail to help me find the money. These problems overcome my naturally weak condition and make me strong! The bigger the problem, the stronger I become! And now, I would like nothing better than a plate of rice *a la Milanese* and a glass of cool beer!"[15]

Frances marveled at the beauty of nature. On her many voyages across the ocean, she was fascinated by the sea. During the day she stood by the stern for hours and at night she stayed out on the deck until 11:00 p.m. gazing at the "sparkling phosphorescence of the sea. It looked," she wrote, "like so many lanterns of a thousand colors on the waves round the ship."[16]

"Daughters," she said, "in our mission here we will find more who will be with us than against us. We shall produce the beautiful fruit of Christ's love in America. We must be aware of two temptations, that of failure and that of success; and often prosperity will be more dangerous than adversity. The money that is the immigrants' blood and tears converted into the gold of banks must be redirected to labor for their well being. With the love of Christ, the earth's wealth of this new field shall be as servant to its soul."[17]

"Love is not loved, my daughters!" she wrote. "Love is not loved!... If we do not burn with love, we do not deserve the title which ennobles us, elevates us, makes us great, and even a portent to the angels in heaven."[18]

Discussion Starters

1. What is your reaction to Frances Cabrini's love for children, especially poor, immigrant children? What can you do to care for poor, abandoned, abused, addicted, and neglected children in your neighborhood and/or in the world?

2. If all people in our world were to embrace one another as sisters and brothers, what difference would this make in our times? How would this affect our ability to share resources? cease wars? make peace? live justly? love God?

3. What impact does Frances Cabrini's missionary vision have on Christians today? How do you react to Pope Pius XII's statement: "Although her constitution was very frail, her spirit was endowed with such singular strength that, knowing the will of God in her regard, she permitted nothing to impede her from accomplishing what seemed beyond the strength of a woman?" Where do you see this attitude reflected in the Church today?

4. How do you connect or bond with Frances Cabrini?

Prayer Experience

1. Find a quiet place and become comfortable. Become attentive to your body... Wiggle your toes, move your feet and legs slowly, tap your fingers, feel your muscles, listen to your heartbeat, journey to your spiritual center...

2. Be aware of your uniqueness and of God's presence dwelling with your physical being... Now look into a mirror for a few minutes and gaze lovingly at your body from head to toe... As you do so, be aware that you are a powerful reflection of God's love...

3. Name, affirm, and give thanks for your uniqueness and specialness... Name special things about you that are gifts from God...

4. See yourself acting as if you are a powerful reflection of God's love to the powerless: high-risk children, people who are foreigners, people with disabilities, people who are sick and aging...people who have been abandoned and forgotten by society...

5. Reflect on Saint Frances Cabrini's words and witness...Write a dialogue with her about what most impresses, intrigues, or challenges you about her story.

6. Find or in some way create a symbol, image, or color that expresses your vision for changing society.

7. Share your symbol with a significant other in your life, such as a friend, a spiritual director, a spouse, a faith community. Decide on

one practical thing that you can do to live out your vision to help the powerless in your area. Invite others to join you in this venture.

Awaiting the
Vision

doris Klein CSJ

16.

Therese of Lisieux

Image of God's Passionate Love

On October 9, 1997, Pope John Paul II officially proclaimed Saint Therese of Lisieux to be a Doctor of the Church. She is the third woman in the history of the Church to receive this honor. Catherine of Siena and Teresa of Avila are the other two.

Therese was born into a devout Catholic family in Alencon, a small town in Normandy, France, on January 2, 1873. She was the ninth and last child of Louis and Zelie Martin.

Therese's spiritual autobiography, *Story of a Soul,* provides glimpses into her earliest memories of a warm loving, family life: "Through the whole of my life God has been pleased to surround me with love. My first memories are of smiles and loving caresses.... So I loved Daddy and Mummy very much and, as I was very open-hearted, I showed my love in a thousand ways."[1]

Celebrating the wonders of creation was as natural to Therese as breathing the fresh air around her. On Sundays, when she strolled with her parents through fields of wheat and wildflowers, she felt a special kinship with Earth. "I can still feel the deep emotion I felt when I saw the fields of wheat starred with poppies, cornflowers, and daisies. I was already in love with far distances, with open spaces and with great trees.... Truly the whole world smiled on me."[2]

Therese's First Communion was one of the most important spiritual events of her life. "The time of my first communion remains engraved in my heart as a memory without clouds.... Ah how sweet was the first kiss of Jesus! It was a kiss of love; I felt I was loved, and I said; 'I love you and I give myself to you forever!'"[3]

Therese was an anxious child. At the time of preparation for her second communion, Therese was overwhelmed by scruples. Marie, her sister, listened compassionately to Therese's repetition of her faults and failures. Therese recalls the torment that she experienced. Sometimes she would cry if she offended someone she loved, and would cry again for having cried. At Midnight Mass in 1886, she experienced a heart healing that would change her life.

According to her family tradition, the children left their shoes near the fireplace on Christmas Eve. Then, after Midnight Mass, Therese and her sisters would excitedly remove their presents from their shoes. On this particular evening, as she ran upstairs to prepare for this eagerly anticipated event, Therese overheard her father telling her older sister, Celine, that he hoped this would be the last time he would have to put small gifts in his youngest daughter's shoes. Tears filled Therese's eyes when she heard her father's comment, but after she calmed down, she joyfully removed the presents from her slippers, as if she had not heard her father's words.

In her autobiography, Therese recalled happy memories of sitting on her father's knee as he told stories and sang songs to her. As she rested in his arms, she knew how the saints prayed. "You carried me to bed and I used to say: 'Have I been good today? Are the little angels going to watch over me?' You always said yes...then you and Marie kissed me goodnight."[4]

When Therese was four years old, her mother died, leaving a tremendous void in Therese's life. In her autobiography, she recalled that she did not cry very much, nor did she share the feelings she experienced at this traumatic loss. Her sisters, Pauline and Marie, were like mothers to her, providing her with warmth and affection, and her father adored her, referring to her as his "little queen."

When Pauline entered Carmel on October 2, 1882, once again Therese was devastated and shortly afterwards became seriously ill. Her body shook violently, and she thought this strange illness might be the work of the devil. Her other sisters, Marie, Leonie, and Celine, joined Therese in praying for her recovery. One day as they prayed before a statue of Mary, "Suddenly the Blessed Virgin glowed with a beauty beyond anything I had ever seen. Her face was alive with kindness and an infinite tenderness, but it was her enchanting smile which really moved me to the depths. My pain vanished and two great tears crept down my cheeks—tears of pure joy."[5]

At the age of fourteen, Therese heard the same calling as her sister, Pauline, and desired to enter Carmel. But because of her age, she needed to get permission from her father, from the ecclesiastical superior of the Carmelite Order, and from the bishop. Canon Delatroctte, the ecclesiastical superior of the convent, at first insisted that Therese wait until she was twenty-one years old. Therese then approached the bishop, who warmly received her but told her he would not make a decision until he had consulted with the Carmelite superior.

Therese then decided to go to Rome and request the pope's permission to enter Carmel at the age of fifteen. As Therese knelt before the pontiff imploring his intercession on her behalf, Pope Leo XIII clasped her hands and rested them on his knee. Then gazing into her eyes, he replied that she would enter Carmel if it was God's will. Finally, on New Year's Day 1888, Therese received the long awaited letter of acceptance. Three months later, on April 9, 1888, her dream became a reality. She described the heart-wrenching, beautiful scene: "I kissed all my relatives and knelt before Father to receive his blessing. He knelt himself and blessed me as he wept. To this old man offering God his child, still in the springtime of her life, was a sight to make the angels rejoice. Then at last the doors of Carmel closed behind me and I was embraced by those beloved sisters who had been like mothers to me and by a whole new family whose love and tenderness is little guessed at by the world outside."[6] On that day Therese experienced a deep peace that never left her, even in the midst of great tribulations.

Everything about her Therese's life in Carmel thrilled her. "But the joy I was experiencing was calm, the lightest breeze did not undulate the quiet waters upon which my little boat was floating and no cloud darkened my blue heaven...With what deep joy, I repeated those words: 'I am here forever and ever!'"[7]

Therese's sufferings in religious life came in the form of painful interpersonal relationships with her prioress, novice mistress, and a novice companion, and in the privations of convent living, the illness of her father, and the dryness of her prayer life. In a letter to her sister, Mother Agnes (Therese's older sister, Pauline), Therese described putting up with irritations as a way to spiritual transformation. During meditation, a sister made noises that disturbed Therese's prayer. She wrote: "I tried to love the little noise which was so displeasing; instead of trying not to hear it (impossible), I paid close attention so as to hear it well, as though it were a delightful concert, and my prayer (which was not the Prayer of Quiet) was spent in offering this concert to Jesus."[8]

Therese made her final vows in 1890 and became assistant to the mistress of novices in 1893. In 1895, at the request of her superior, she started to write the story of her childhood, which afterwards was expanded into an autobiography. In 1896 she became ill and died of tuberculosis at the age of twenty-four. She was beatified in 1923 and was canonized by Pope Pius XI two years later, on May 17, 1925.

In an article titled "'Little Flower:' A Likely Doctor of Church for an Age of Anxiety," H. D. Kreilkamp, professor emeritus of history and philosophy at St. Joseph's College in Rensselaer, Indiana, asserts that Therese is a mentor for people today who are stressed over life's uncertainties. He says that her solution to worry is to let go and let God handle it, like a child trusts a loving father. He observes that Therese's love of suffering is not depressing or dark; rather her spirituality affirms that all of life's experiences can lead to integration.[9]

Therese reminds us that God's love is with us always and everywhere, and therefore we have nothing to fear. All we have to do is trust in divine love. God is always there to embrace us, especially through our suffering and pain. Like Therese, we can see suffering as a catalyst for releasing our "survivor gift," and thus helping us respond to life's challenges in spite of our fears. Our sufferings can become pathways to wholeness and holiness. Suffering can become an occasion for us to open our hearts and experience solidarity with all those who suffer throughout the world. Like this newly named Doctor of the Church, we can look on our sufferings as reflections of the power of God at work in every moment of our lives, healing and transforming us. When we have problems with our health, go through a crisis in our jobs, or experience the loss of a loved one, we can rest assured—like Therese—that God is our comfort and support.

Therese's "Little Way" demonstrates that the path to God is often found in hidden, unnoticed details of our lives—like making delicious peanut butter sandwiches for our children day in and day out, cutting the grass for an older neighbor, listening to a friend who has experienced a major loss in her life, loving our spouse, children, and ourselves just as we are, faults and all. Can we, like Therese, live this kind of love? Can we accept the good and the bad, confident that we are loved profoundly and passionately by our God? That's the bottom line of Therese's "Little Way"—complete confidence in God's love. Ultimately that's all that matters. What more do we need?

Reflection

I feel in me the vocation of the priest. With that love, O Jesus, I would carry you in my hands.... And...give you to souls!

Ah! in spite of my littleness, I would like to enlighten souls as did the prophets and the Doctors. I have the vocation of the apostle.... I would want to preach the gospel on all the five continents simultaneously and even to the most remote isles. I would be a missionary, not for a few years only but from the beginning of creation until the consummation of the ages. But above all, O my beloved Savior, I would shed my blood for you even to the very last drop.

Charity gave me the key to my vocation... I understood that the Church had a heart and that this heart was burning with love. I understood it was love alone that made the Church's members act, that if love ever became extinct, apostles would not preach the gospel and martyrs would not shed their blood. I understood that love comprised all vocations, that love was everything, that it embraced all times and places...in a word, that it was eternal!... Then, in the excess of my delirious joy, I cried out: O Jesus, my love...my vocation, at last I have found it.... My vocation is love![10]

Discussion Starters

1. What significance does Therese's call to priesthood have for women in the Church today?

2. How is Therese an image of God's passionate love? Do you see yourself as an image of God's passionate love? What can you do to grow more deeply in God's love?

3. What impact can Therese's "Little Way" have on contemporary Christians?

4. How can our sufferings be transformed into growth? Do you believe that "the resurrection" principle in Christian life works in changing negatives into positives? Explain your understanding of suffering.

Prayer Experience

(You might want to select some classical instrumental music to accompany your prayer experience.)

1. Breathe deeply and slowly for several minutes... Imagine each breath you take is filled with the infinite love of God for you, for all people, for all creation... Breathe in boundless love... Breathe out love eternal...

2. Slowly and thoughtfully reread the Reflection...

3. Imagine you are sitting in the presence of Jesus... Listen as Jesus shares the passionate love he has for you... Ask Jesus a question... Listen for a response... Jesus asks you a question... Hear his words and his gentle voice...

4. Jesus has a special mission for you... Open your heart to your calling, and ponder its meaning in your life...

5. Express gratitude for the gift of divine love that you experience each day... Jesus assures you that you will be given all the love you need to live your calling as a channel of God's glory shining radiantly in the world... Express your trust in God's love to supply all your needs...

6. You are aware that the journey ahead may be full of new challenges, risks, and even rejection... Share your feelings with Jesus... Ask Jesus to help you live as an image of God's passionate love, no matter what obstacles you may face... Open your hands as a sign of

letting go and giving everything to Jesus… Be conscious of the people God is now calling you to love… See yourself walking toward them, with Jesus at your side… You are confident, full of peace and tranquillity… You can do all things in Jesus who strengthens you…

7. Be conscious that the spirit of Therese of Lisieux accompanies you as you live your commitment to be a reflection of Jesus to everyone you meet… She is your soul companion who is always there to encourage you and cheer you on as you live your vocation to love… Let her words resound in your soul this day: "O Jesus, my love…my vocation, at last I have found it… My vocation is love!" Express your commitment in your own words to love freely, joyously, and passionately…

Led by the
Vision

17.

Dorothy Day

Exemplar of Peace and Justice

On November 9, 1997, the day after the world celebrated the centennial of Dorothy Day's birth, Cardinal John O'Connor of New York announced that he would propose her as a candidate for sainthood. Why has Dorothy Day had such a profound impact on our world, so much so that just seventeen years after her death, a Church leader would champion her cause as a saintly role model for our times? To answer this question, we need only reflect on her life.

Dorothy Day, the third child of Grace Satteall and John I. Day, was born in Brooklyn, New York, on November 8, 1897. Her father was a journalist, and Dorothy shared his love for the written word. "We all liked to write," she reminisced, "and I had been taught early to write personally, subjectively about what I saw around me and what was being done."[1]

As a sports writer, John Day frequently moved his family across the country, which interrupted Dorothy's friendships and deepened her sense of loneliness. Yet Dorothy remembered her childhood as a happy time, and the solitude as a positive factor in her life: "It seems that I spent much time alone in spite of the fact that I had two brothers and a sister. There was joy in being alone and I can remember happy hours."[2]

In an attempt to protect the innocence of his children, John Day restricted the family's exposure to the outside world. Reading was one of the few pastimes allowed in the Day home. Although Dorothy later overcame these restrictions, they were formative in her character development. As Mel Piehl notes: "There would always remain for her an old-fashioned longing for the security of a home and loving family, a tendency that seemed to contradict her equally strong inclinations in its rebelliousness and defiance of social convention.[3]

Dorothy's mother, Grace, was the power that kept the family connected and secure. Although reserved like her husband, Grace displayed affection to her children; no bedtime was without mother's kiss. During times of financial hardship she managed to bring her family through. Years later Dorothy recalled the strength her mother showed during difficult times, a skill that impressed her young daughter. Dorothy recalled that at the end of a particularly bad day, her mother would take a bath, dress in her loveliest clothes, seat her children around the table, and entertain—as if she were hosting a special party.

In 1906 the Day family lived in San Francisco during the earthquake that destroyed much of the city, including her father's newspaper building. Dorothy never forgot the caring that her mother and her neighbors showed in serving the homeless at that time. After this catastrophe the family moved to Chicago, where John Day went to work for the *Chicago Inter Ocean*—and the family settled into a middle-class lifestyle.

The Day home was not one in which religion or God was discussed. At the urging of a rector of the local Episcopal church, however, Grace allowed her sons to join the choir and Dorothy to attend the Sunday liturgy. Dorothy was deeply touched by the Episcopal rituals and prayers, especially the psalms. Her first exposure to Roman Catholicism came through observing Mrs. Barrett, a friend's mother, at prayer. As she observed the woman's devotions, Dorothy experienced "a warm burst of love," as she later put it.[4]

At sixteen Dorothy attended the University of Illinois, but left college at nineteen to live in New York and work as a reporter for a socialist paper. Her writings reflect her sense of justice and the desire to change the poverty she saw all around her after World War I. She reported on labor meetings, protests, and strikes, criticizing the disparity between the classes.

During these years Dorothy drifted from place to place: Europe, Chicago, New Orleans, and California. She also drifted from relationship to relationship. She fell in love with Lionel Moise, became pregnant, and had an abortion. Soon after this she married Berkeley Tobey and traveled to Europe with him. After their return home, however, they broke off the relationship.

Dorothy's first jail experience occurred when she joined a group of suffragists at the White House to protest the despicable treatment of other suffragists in jail. She joined the hunger strike with the other women protesters and observed the violent abuse that human beings are capable of inflicting on one another. "Never would I recover from this wound," she said later; "this ugly knowledge I had gained...It was one thing to be writing about these things, to have the theoretical knowledge of sweatshops and injustice and hunger, but it was quite another to experience it in one's own flesh."[5]

In 1925 Dorothy fell in love with Forestor Batterham, entered into a common-law marriage, and had a child with him. This was a time of natural happiness for Dorothy, but in the midst of her joy she realized something was missing. "It was a peace curiously enough divided against itself. I was happy, but my very happiness made me know that there was a greater happiness to be obtained from life than I had ever known."[6] It was a time when she began to pray more and pursue a spiritual meaning of life.

When her daughter, Tamar Teresa, was born, Dorothy decided to have the baby baptized in the Roman Catholic Church because she did not want her child to grow up the way she had, without a religious foundation. Although a loving father, Forester was an atheist and opposed to any Church or state interference that might result in the validation of their marriage. This put Dorothy in the position of choosing to continue living with him or to become a Catholic, since she knew her step toward organized religions was one Forester could never accept. She chose her newfound faith, but not without grief and heartbreak.

In 1932 the Catholic magazine, *Commonweal,* commissioned Dorothy to write an article about a march organized by Communists who were challenging legislators to make laws that would benefit workers and their families. Dorothy described her mixed emotions as she watched the marchers: "I stood on the curb and watched them, joy and pride in the courage of this band of men and women mounting in my heart, and with a bitterness too that since I was now a Catholic, with fundamental philosophical differences, I could not be out there with them. I could write; I could protest, to arouse the conscience; but where was the Catholic leadership in the gathering of bands of men and women together for the actual works of mercy that the comrades had always made part of their technique in reaching the workers?"[7]

When she returned to New York, Dorothy met Peter Maurin, from whom she came to understand the social teachings of Catholicism. Together they started the Catholic Worker Movement and the penny newspaper that would become its trademark. They named the paper *The Catholic Worker,* and sold it for a penny a copy because many Catholics during this era were destitute and exploited. At the end of the first year, the circulation of the paper was 100,000. Together Dorothy and Peter opened their "houses of hospitality" to feed the hungry and help the unemployed who came to them. Dorothy wrote about the plight of the poor and the abysmal conditions that workers and the labor movement faced in attempting to bring about change.

Catholic Worker houses spread around the country, and Catholic Workers participated in strikes, pickets, boycotts, and protests to change low wages and poor working conditions. Dorothy and Peter shared their belief that work should be creative, not dehumanizing. They were as much soul brother and sister as mentor and disciple, and when Peter Maurin died in 1949, Dorothy experienced a tremendous grief. The work of the Movement continued, however, and was a prophetic voice for justice and equality in the civil rights movement, a supporter of nonviolence, and a voice for the ban on nuclear weapons.

Dorothy was jailed many times during these years, always because she spoke up for the gospel. She was arrested and sent to jail for the last time in 1973, when she joined Caesar Chavez and the United Farm Workers in the San Joaquin Valley in a nonviolent demonstration against the Teamsters Union. After that her health began to deteriorate but, even though she suffered from a heart condition, she continued to write and speak about her work on behalf of justice and peace. She suffered a major heart attack in 1976 and died four years later, on November 29, 1980. He daughter, Tamar, was at her side.

Dorothy Day was an active contemplative with a prophetic passion for justice—one who "did her theology" before the phrase became popular. As Robert Coles puts it in his biography of Day: "She was an earthy, political, practical-minded person, yet she could be almost willfully blind to the world's habits and priorities as she persisted in the direction of her faith."[8]

On the occasion of the centenary celebration of Dorothy Day's birth, Robert Ellsberg enunciated the three great gifts he believes were Dorothy's legacy to the world: her wedding of the everyday corporal works of mercy to her commitment to justice; her acts of civil disobedience as a critique of society's inability to transform the structures needed for systemic change; and her struggle to live the gospel vision of nonviolence, which expanded the Church's understanding of love for enemies in a modern context. All this is seen as part and parcel of Dorothy's particular call to holiness.[9]

Dorothy Day had a passion for justice. She believed that Christ came to give abundant life to everyone, especially to the poor. In her we have an icon of the poor Christ who calls us to feed the hungry, clothe the naked, shelter the homeless. Dorothy challenges us to love our enemies and treat one another fairly and justly. Caring for the destitute, while confronting the system that makes them poor, was at the heart of Dorothy's witness to the gospel and the social teachings of the Church. In her own life, she lived simply, embracing voluntary poverty so that others could simply live.

The fire that ignited Dorothy Day's soul has spread not only through Catholic Workers but also through countless people around the world who act on behalf of justice and peace, one small step at a time, one day at a time. Dorothy Day is a contemporary activist we can identify with. She is a woman who, like us, was very human and very determined. She was a twentieth-century prophet who challenged racism, violence, militarism, sexism, capitalism, and all kinds of exploitation. Like every prophet, she was criticized for resisting the status quo and yet, ironically, she was merely enfleshing the papal encyclicals on justice (*Rerum Novarum* and *Quadragestino Anno*). Years later the U.S. bishops echoed the same principles that Dorothy had stood for when they issued their pastoral letters on peace, the economy, and women's concerns.

Dorothy Day is a goad to our middle-class consciences. She radiates the mind of Christ, which reiterates that we are our sisters' and brothers' keepers. She shows us the face of Christ in every bag lady, derelict, and protester we attempt to ignore. She also reminds us that our small acts of caring and our simplest efforts to foster justice do make a difference.

Like Dorothy, we can begin right now. We don't have to wait until we have it all together to join with others in the pursuit of peace and justice. As a pacifist, Dorothy lived the Sermon on the Mount and showed us how to deal with conflict and violence in our society in a positive nonviolent way. Her witness challenges conservatives and liberals in Church and society to cut out the uselessness of finger pointing and blaming, and get to the work of dialoguing with one another openly and honestly to discover common ground. Her voluntary poverty calls us to lighten up, get rid of our excessive material things, and give our resources of time and love to those who need them most. When we do this, we will, like Dorothy, experience the abundant life Christ came to share with all people. Our little spark, lit from hers, can light a fire. If, like Dorothy, we are criticized, even persecuted, for our beliefs and actions on behalf of a more just world, we will know we are really on track.

Perhaps the time is now to be prophetic activists who believe and live the gospel right where we are. At the dawning of the twenty-first century Christ is calling us to be consumed with a blazing passion for justice. And God's justice is total mercy! Then in the star-studded nights, we, too, like "Saint Dorothy Day," will shine like stars.

Reflection

And the loveliest of all relationships in Christ's life, after his relationship with his mother, is his relationship with Martha, Mary and Lazarus and the continued hospitality he found with them. It is a staggering thought that there were once two sisters and a brother whom Jesus looked on almost as his family and where he found a second home.

If we hadn't got Christ's own words for it, it would seem raving lunacy to believe that if I offer a bed and food and hospitality to some man, woman or child, I am replaying the part of Lazarus or Martha or Mary and my guest is Christ.

We can do it too, exactly as they did. We are not born too late. We do it by seeing Christ and serving Christ in friends and strangers, in everyone we come in contact with.[10]

Discussion Starters

1. What is the legacy of Dorothy Day for the Church and the world?

2. In what situations can you practice hospitality to family? friends? strangers? Is Christ calling you to live the gospel vision of justice more intentionally at this time? How can you be a change agent for social justice in our world today? What support system will you need in order to do this?

3. Describe your understanding of what a passion for justice would mean for you, the Church, the world.

4. How are Martha, Mary, and Lazarus models of hospitality for contemporary Christians? How do we know Christ, one another, and ourselves in the breaking of bread? How can we experience love through

community? What implications does this kind of sharing have in developing a eucharistic spirituality?

Prayer Experience

1. Take a few slow, deep abdominal breaths... Focus your attention on breathing slowly and deeply... Breathe in deeply through your nose... Breathe out gently through your mouth... As you concentrate on your breathing, imagine a beautiful, flaming light rising up in front of your body... As you exhale, watch it move down your head...your shoulders...your chest...your spine...your abdomen... your arms...your legs... Feel your entire body fill with this beautiful, flaming light...

2. Slowly and prayerfully, reread the Reflection...

3. Close your eyes and travel back to the time of Jesus... See yourself sitting around the table in the home of Mary, Martha, and Lazarus... See Dorothy Day at the table with you... Hear all the laughter and the wonderful stories everyone is telling...You feel relaxed and welcome as you break bread and drink wine together... Feel the love present in the room... Feel it fill you with energy and enthusiasm... Realize that you have questions and ideas—and plenty of time to share... Feel the challenge ahead of you... Feel affirmed by the message Jesus has for you... Connect deeply with your soul sister, Dorothy... Understand the power of her determined and stubborn love to set the world on fire for justice, peace, and equality... Stay as long as you can in the presence of this small community...

4. Now imagine yourself around a table talking to your own family and close friends... Be conscious of your feelings... As you look at each one, see Christ... As you listen to each one, hear Christ... As

you touch each one, embrace Christ... If there is anyone missing from this table, ask yourself why you are estranged, for this is your initial step into the issue of peace and justice—the peace and justice of Jesus... Decide now to begin to bridge the gap...

5. Now see yourself living through a typical day... Be aware of how you would approach each person...each task...each event... Imagine Christ everywhere you go... Be aware that Christ is loving others through you in everything you say and do...

6. Now see yourself, with your family, working for and sharing with the poor and needy in your neighborhood... Ask each person how you can serve him or her... Be aware that each one is Christ...each person is a member of your family...your sister...your brother...who provides a glimpse into the heart of God... Invite each person to speak the truth in love to you...to convert you to a deeper understanding of the Poor Christ in the gospel...

7. Imagine yourself joining with others to work for change and transformation of unjust laws and structures that cause poverty, injustice, and violence in our world... Believe that you can make a difference... Consider what you might be called to do... Contemplate your dreams for the global healing of humanity... Imagine yourself daring to work with others who share a similar vision... See yourself consumed with a blazing passion for God's justice—which is mercy—a passion like "Saint Dorothy's"...

Delighting in the Vision

18.

Catherine de Hueck Doherty

Witness to Gospel Living

Catherine de Hueck was born on a train in Nijni-Novgorod, Russia, on August 15, 1900—a result of her mother's miscalculation. As soon as her child was born, Catherine's mother worried that her child might catch a disease. Thus she insisted that Catherine be baptized on the same day, in a Russian Orthodox church, because there was no Roman Catholic church in the city at that time.

Catherine was born to a wealthy family, with fourteen people in domestic service to the large household. As a child, however, Catherine was not pampered. Her mother made sure that Catherine learned how to sew, cook, and clean—everything that the domestics did—under the supervision of the professional staff. Catherine remembered her learning experiences: "When my time in the kitchen ended I was transferred to the laundry; when I finished there I became the housemaid.... My waiting on the family was often punctuated by such helpful, joking remarks as, 'Don't get the gravy down my neck'; 'Hold it straight'; 'Follow the butler and don't get ahead of him'; 'Don't rush people.'"[1]

In her autobiography titled *Fragments of My Life,* Catherine described a humorous memory from her childhood that occurred around the time her family got electricity installed in their house. When Catherine kept pushing the switch up and down, as children love to do, her mother warned her to stop. When Catherine wouldn't obey, she was punished by being put in a corner. Catherine recalled: "With my nose between two walls, I cogitated—philosophized! I must have been there 15 minutes when mother called, 'You can come out now.' I said, 'I haven't finished thinking.' So she left me there. Finally I was ready. I said, 'Mother, I think I'll go to grandmother's house. I don't feel comfortable around here!' or words to that effect. 'Furthermore,' I said, 'you can have my dolls!'"[2]

Catherine's father worked in the service of the czar, which meant that the family traveled to Egypt, France, Turkey, and various other places. Catherine recalled that when the family was stationed in Egypt, they would attend Holy Week services in Jerusalem. Her mother, a Russian Orthodox, loved the liturgies of the Church, especially the burial of Christ. Her father, a Roman Catholic, was particularly mindful of the abandonment of Christ in the Garden of Gethsemane, and so would always bring home from there a large container of the blessed olive oil. It's easy to see how Catherine inherited her deep devotion to the passion of Christ from her parents.[3]

At the age of fifteen, Catherine married Baron Boris de Hueck, an artist and engineer. In 1917, after the October Revolution, the young couple suffered semi-starvation, the fear of Communist persecution, and the ravages of civil war. The days following the Bolshevik Revolution were horrible ones for Boris and Catherine. Most of their wealth was confiscated by the Bolshevik army. When they returned to their plundered apartment, they packed the few things that had not been taken, slipped down the stairs of the apartment, opened the door quietly so as not to be discovered, and fled.

The couple walked a great distance, until they crossed into Finland and arrived at a villa owned by their family—only to discover that the Communists had taken possession of the area. They became virtual prisoners in their own home. Catherine remembered: "They are in a room with a fireplace, a few forgotten, frozen potatoes, and a couple of windows from which their tormentors are able to watch them slowly starve to death. This ordeal lasts some two weeks."[4]

Shortly afterward, the White Army freed them and Catherine and Boris journeyed to Murmansk and later took a ship to England; they were refugees. They had escaped from Russia with only the clothes on their back.

Finally, in 1920, they arrived in Halifax and took the train to Toronto, where they received a warm welcome. However, life was challenging. Catherine was pregnant and Boris was sick. Catherine supported the family by being a waitress, a store clerk, and a laundress—doing whatever work she could find. In 1921 her son, George Theodore Mario, was born. Fortunately Boris eventually recuperated and was hired by the Dominion Factory Company in Montreal.

During this time Catherine and Boris experienced marital problems. Later Catherine reflected on the painful loss of her marriage: "Love dies slowly if it dies at all. There were many difficult days between Boris and me. My life with him was very strange. I always tried to forgive and forget…But the source of this love that I had for him—did it shrivel up? Did it just go into a corner someplace in my heart and hide itself there? I don't know…. But I knew that something was happening to me and my love for Boris. Eventually, at the advice of a Jesuit priest, our marriage was annulled."[5]

Within a few years Catherine became known as a talented public speaker. She obtained a job as a lecturer for a bureau, earning her a good salary; later she would become an executive for this bureau. Consequently she was able to afford a spacious apartment, childcare for her son, and a comfortable car. But in the midst of her success, Catherine felt a strong call to serve the poor. The words of Christ in the gospel kept coming back to her: "Sell all that you own and distribute the money to the poor, and you will have treasure in heaven; then, come, follow me" (Luke 18:22).

Catherine tried to push this idea from her mind but the nagging thought continued. She prayed for guidance and finally sought direction from the archbishop of Toronto, Neil McNeil. He affirmed her vocation and advised her to pray for another year. At the end of that time, after providing for her son's education, Catherine decided to sell everything she had, give the money to the poor, and live the gospel in the midst of the poor people of Toronto. There she founded the first Friendship House.[6]

Catherine always knew that she wanted to live simply and minister to the needy. She recalled a childhood memory in which she would pray at a Saint Francis shrine in the yard of Our Lady of Zion Convent School in Ramleh-Alexandria, Egypt. She was particularly impressed by the stories the teacher told about the saint, and decided that she wanted to emulate him by living among the poor. Her childhood dream became a reality years later when, joined by a few companions, she started Friendship House.[7]

At the invitation of Father John LaFarge, Catherine moved to Harlem, New York. It was February 14, 1938, and with only a small suitcase, a typewriter, and a few dollars in her purse, she began her work for racial justice. In Harlem Catherine often dreamed of being Black. She read and reread John Howard Griffin's book *Black Like Me*. She wrote: "He had embodied my dream. It was such a pain to me that I couldn't become black."[8] Catherine was outraged at the discrimination against Blacks that she found among ministers of the gospel in Harlem. She believed that it was wrong for Christians—let alone ministers—to be biased.[9]

When Catherine lectured in the South on racial justice, people would physically attack her, tearing her clothes and throwing rotten eggs, tomatoes, and cabbage. On one occasion, when people cautioned her not to go to the South, she replied: "If you are going to preach the Gospel with your life, you have to preach it everywhere. You can't say, I'll preach it in New York but not in Georgia."[10]

Catherine's interracial work flourished in New York and soon spread to Chicago, Washington, and Portland. She was well received by some in the American Church, but others had difficulty understanding her vision. Some people did not appreciate her honesty or openness. Because of differences of opinion about the nature of Friendship House, Catherine found herself having to move again. Like Dorothy Day, making the Church's social teachings a living reality rather than letting them remain simple documents that were read infrequently was challenging work.[11]

In 1943 Catherine married Eddie Doherty, a newspaper journalist. Four years later, in 1947, at the invitation of the bishop of Pembroke, the couple moved to Combermere, Ontario, a small rural village one hundred and eighty miles from Toronto, to serve the poor in rural Canada. On their first day there, they planted apple trees. Even though things did not go smoothly at first, and they were tempted to give up, they stayed—and God blessed them as others joined their efforts. Their ministry eventually developed into the Madonna House apostolate, a diocesan union of laity and priests who desired to live the gospel together and to share Christian love with others.

In 1955 Catherine and Eddie made vows of celibacy and in 1969, Eddie was ordained a priest in the Melkite Rite. The 60s and 70s were fruitful years for the community and for Catherine. In October 1976, Catherine had a dream in which her mother appeared to her and told her that God wanted her to write. During the next ten years, she wrote books, lectured extensively, did TV and radio interviews, and was consulted by many people from all over the world. Then, after a long illness, Catherine died peacefully on December 14, 1985.[12]

Reflecting on the profound impact of Catherine's spirituality, Father Robert D. Pelton wrote: "As she has moved, the Spirit has cast that fire about her on every side. Her pilgrimage has always been also a standing still in the center of her own heart, 'where,' she says, 'all in me is silent and where I am immersed in the silence of God.'"[13]

Catherine believed that the gospel of Jesus Christ was the only real revolution the world has ever experienced. Jesus guided Catherine from a peaceful childhood, through horrible deprivation in the midst of violent persecution and war, to a new land and a new calling. In the midst of the suffering and uncertainty she faced, Catherine's faith did not waver. Here she dwelt in the *poustinia* of her own heart. "Poustinia" is the journey of the soul that is open to all who desire it.

Like Catherine, we need to discover our still point where we can be anchored in God. At our still point, nothing can uproot us or destroy our peace of soul, even as we live the counter-cultural commitment of the gospel. When we live like Jesus, Catherine reminds us, we will find poverty, freedom, and defenselessness. Here also, she adds, we will experience "cosmic tenderness" in all creatures, in our sisters and brothers, and in ourselves.[14] Then as we discover the power of Christ dwelling within us and all around us, we will become reflections of the joy of God. This is where gospel living leads us. What more could we want!

In recent years the numbers and missions of Madonna House have grown and flourished to approximately two hundred members (nine staff and applicants). About one hundred live in Combermere, Ontario, Canada, and the rest serve in twenty-two houses located in the U.S., Canada, West Indies, England, France, Brazil, and Africa. Some of these houses serve the material needs of the surrounding populations; others are "listening houses" that minister to loneliness which, according to Catherine, is the greatest poverty of our time. In each Madonna House the primary call is to create a community of love, to offer hospitality of the heart and home, and to witness to gospel living.[15] What a powerful tribute to a woman with a vision.

Reflection

I am sitting at the very edge of the pine forest, looking down. Suddenly I am not there at all. I am where my heart has always been. I am with the poor. Such a love, such a joy, such a simple, childlike joy, fills my heart, and I keep repeating to myself, "I am with the poor. I am descending from the holy mountain to go to them." And the wind that is always around the holy mountain tells me, "No. No. They are coming to you." I say to myself, "If they are coming to me, I must make a feast. I must feed them and clothe them and help them in some way."[16]

No, I didn't cry this time. I just stood there, among the poor, and suddenly all of them—Chicanos, other minority groups, Blacks—suddenly they became Christ, the powerful, beautiful Christ.[17]

Discussion Starters

1. Catherine de Hueck Doherty reminds us that the poor reflect "the powerful, beautiful Christ." How do the poor reveal Christ to the world today?

2. How can you share with the poor? Why is this important?

3. How does gospel living challenge us? Why is this important?

4. How can you live a simple lifestyle so that others can simply live? What can society do to empower the poor? How can you participate in this work?

Prayer Experience

1. Get as comfortable as you can in your chair, on a cushion, or in your favorite prayer position... Take a few, slow, deep abdominal breaths... Allow your body to breathe according to its own natural rhythm...slowly...deeply...easily...

2. As you focus on your breathing, imagine a warm golden light moving from the top of your head to the soles of your feet each time you inhale and exhale... Imagine this warm light moving through every cell of your body... This healing light touches and heals every part of your body...your mind...your spirit...

3. In your imagination form a picture or image of God in the poor of the Earth...in all your sisters and brothers...in all creatures...in

you… Express in words, impressions, or pictures anything you are aware of.

4. Reflect on Catherine de Hueck Doherty's life…her theology…her spirituality…her prayer…her humility…her detachment from material things…her poverty of spirit…her love for the poor…her joy in gospel living…

5. Invite the Holy One to speak to you through your thoughts, feelings, body sensations, images, intuitions, etc.… Offer thanks for the poor, "the powerful, beautiful Christ" in our midst…

6. Contemplate your oneness with all people and the Earth… Imagine a healing, sparkling, golden, light whirling through time and space…through you…through the poor…through all human persons…through all creatures…bringing justice, liberation, and peace everywhere… Feel surrounded by the love radiating from this divine light…

7. Open yourself to the embrace of Cosmic Tenderness… Let go of all your barriers… Let go of all your prejudices… Let go of all your biases… Be conscious of your oneness with the poor…the rejected…the destitute…the lonely…the alienated…the forgotten members of society… Be aware of your oneness with all these in the arms of divine love… Listen to the voices of the poor, your sisters and brothers from every nation, creed, race, ethnic background, and generation… Be aware that they have an important message for you…for humanity… Invite the poor to teach you about their needs …their human dignity…their experiences of life on our common home, Earth… Reflect on how you can live the gospel more fully… Decide on one way you will serve those in need.

Nurturing
the
Vision

Doris Klein CSA

19.

Jean Donovan

Martyr for Justice,
Model of Woman-Strength

O n the night Jean Donovan was killed, her mother, Pat, remembers: "I was up all night. I had this terrible feeling that if she didn't come home, something terrible was going to happen to her. And I kept begging God to bring Jeannie home."[1] Three days later, Pat and her husband, Ray, were informed that the bodies of four Church women—Jean Donovan, Ita Ford, Maura Clarke, and Dorothy Kazel—had been found in a shallow grave at the side of a dirt road. They had been sexually assaulted and shot.[2]

Jean's life, even more than her senseless death, altered the lives of her parents forever. Pat reflects on the legacy left behind by her daughter: "It's a reversal: Instead of the parents being the role model, the child is."[3]

Although faith or religion was seldom discussed in the Donovan family, the witness of faith permeated every aspect of life. "I felt," as Pat says, "that the children could learn as much by seeing an example. And it must have worked, because they were very active in the church. Michael, the older of the two children, was an altar boy and Jeannie, always the first one up to the altar rail, thought it was terrible that they didn't have altar girls."[4]

After Jean's death, Ray, Pat, and Michael, along with the families of the other slain women, began the long years of frustrating and discouraging work to bring the killers to trial. In the course of this eventual three-and-a-half-year process, Pat and Ray came to recalibrate their opinion of their own government. Pat points out that a few weeks before his inauguration, President-elect Reagan sent the message to the Salvadoran government that, when he became president, Salvador would get all aid needed from the U.S. to fight the rebels and that human rights violations would no longer be an obstacle to obtaining this aid. "This happened, and it broadcast all over El Salvador that human rights violations no longer meant anything, and two weeks later Jean, Dorothy, Ita, and Maura were dead. I can't help but make a connection."[5]

The Salvadoran government tried to cover up the roles that higher officials played in this crime. In fact, there was little movement at all toward a trial until Congress passed a law withholding thirty percent of authorized military aid until there was a verdict in this case. Only then did preparations for a trial progress quickly. Finally, in May 1984, five National Guardsmen were found guilty in the killing of the four women. This was the first time that the Salvadoran security forces were convicted of a politically motivated murder, in spite of the fact that there were more than forty thousand civilians murdered in that country since October 1979.[6]

Despite the conviction and sentencing of the soldiers, many people, including former U.S. Ambassador to Salvador, Robert White, continued to believe that the U.S. government had participated in a cover-up of the truth. There were still many unanswered questions: Who ordered the deaths of the women? How much did the U.S. government know and conceal about the incident?

Ray recalls that in 1986, the government "made a big fanfare [because] they were releasing 480 documents or something like that, and I got a big carton.... [On] every one of those documents...everything was blacked out except 'Dear Sir' and 'Very truly yours,' so they've just been playing games, and I'm sure that these documents would implicate all kinds of people."[7]

News of El Salvador and hints of conspiracies and cover-ups continued to swirl and dominate the news long after the incident. Several articles about the tragedy appeared soon after Jean's death and, in December 1982, a film titled "Roses in December" was aired on PBS. This program raised public consciousness about human rights, oppression, U.S. policy, and gospel values in El Salvador. As a result of the publicity, Pat and Ray received numerous invitations to participate on the lecture circuit, and they have taken that opportunity to advance Jean's work for justice. Usually they begin their talks by showing "Roses in December." Ray then gives an update on the state of affairs in El Salvador, and Pat talks about Jean as a person and the impact her ministry has had on her family and on people of conscience throughout the world.

Instead of benignly accepting everything the government determines, Ray and Pat now ask questions and challenge U.S. government policies. "The day when oppressed people are going to continue living the way they have is just about over," Ray observes. "The winds of change are blowing. Look at El Salvador, Nicaragua, Argentina, the Philippines, South Africa—all over the world people are rising up.... What we've been doing is spending billions of dollars trying to keep the oppressors in power.... And it is a fruitless task—it's not going to work."[8]

Pat and Ray are proud to share the story of their courageous daughter who grew up in a supportive, loving family atmosphere. They gave Jean and her brother, Michael, roots and wings, a solid foundation, and spiritual values that strengthened them. Theirs was a healthy, happy family life.

A fun-loving child and a natural achiever, Jean excelled in her studies and enjoyed a number of hobbies, such as horseback riding. She received a scholarship to Case Western Reserve University and earned a master's degree in economics. At the age of twenty-four, Jean was on the fast track to success as a prominent executive with a well-known Cleveland accounting firm.

Jean was a vivacious, carefree, and spiritual young woman. In her third year of college, she attended the University of Cork in Ireland, as an exchange student. There she met Father Michael Crowley, who was to become a friend and confidant and who encouraged her to become involved in ministry to the poor in Cork. Years later, in 1977, she had the occasion to revisit Cork and to discuss with Father Crowley the direction that her life had been taking. Crowley's insightful comment caused Jean to reflect on her future: "You've got everything. You should think about giving a little back to God."[9]

After her return to Cleveland, Jean volunteered to spend her free time working with inner-city youth. Later that year she learned of a Cleveland diocesan team of volunteers involved in ministry in El Salvador, loosely aligning themselves with the Maryknoll missionaries in the area. Her mother recalls that Jean had discussed her interest in becoming a missionary shortly after her experience in Cork. Skeptical family and friends, however, concluded that the lifestyle would be "at odds with the fun-loving, motorcycle-riding Jean they knew."[10]

The requirements for becoming a lay missionary included a four-month training program at the Maryknoll Center in Ossining, New York, followed by three months of studying Spanish in Guatemala. In 1978 Jean was accepted into the four-month program. Then, upon completion of these courses, Jean said goodbye to her family and close friends, and joined the mission team in El Salvador.

When Jean arrived in La Libertad on August 10, 1979, church bells were tolling in memory of a local priest who had been murdered at the altar of his church. Parishioners who had been present recognized the killers as members of the police force. This incident was Jean's introduction to the harsh realities of death squads and murder in this strife-torn land.[11]

Soon after her arrival in El Salvador, Jean met and teamed up with Ursuline Sister Dorothy Kazel, a veteran missionary in the area. At first she served in an accounting capacity, managing the financial affairs of the mission. But her first significant project was to help administer a food distribution program in a town called Santa Cruz. There she listened to the stories of the peasants and comforted the families whose loved ones had been murdered or who had disappeared. Jean found it fulfilling to be able to help people who were hurting.

As the political situation in El Salvador worsened, Church workers began planning refugee centers, but they attempted to keep an atmosphere of calm by teaching religious education classes, conducting religious services, providing health services, and distributing food. The summer after Jean arrived, the mission team began to include recovery and burial of the bodies of the victims of death squads as part of their work. At this time Jean and her associates became alarmed by the violence and reprisals against native clergy and Church workers that were becoming daily realities.[12]

Some Church leaders preached courageously about the injustices that the poor people of El Salvador suffered. It was Archbishop Oscar Romero, however, who spoke passionately and publicly about the atrocities that were taking place: "There is a terrible situation among the poor—they are crushed in their homes, taken prisoners, made to disappear. They go to jail, are judged falsely and no one pays any attention. I felt I had to be the voice of all those people without a voice."[13] The peasants were affirmed and uplifted by Romero's sermons, broadcast every Sunday. Jean also was encouraged by the archbishop's sermons on those infrequent occasions when she could attend his service.

Suffering the same fate as those he preached about, Archbishop Romero was shot to death at the alter while celebrating the Eucharist on March 24, 1980. His funeral, which Jean attended, was marked by further violence and death. For many people even today, nearly twenty years later, the spirit of Oscar Romero still lives in the Salvadoran people. The blood of martyrs is indeed the seed of faith.

Murder had become commonplace in El Salvador and, when Jean learned that some members of the Santa Cruz community had been bludgeoned to death, she became uneasy about her own safety. This was followed by yet another terrifying incident. On July 6, after an evening at the movies, Jean and two male Salvadoran friends had just said goodnight. As she entered her apartment, Jean heard gunshots and, running back out, found her two friends dead on the street.[14] Jean was shocked and grieved over the loss of her associates, but kept up her own efforts to work with the poor. She and Dorothy moved refugees to safe centers as well as provided food and supplies for them as needed.

In August, Maryknoll sisters Ita and Carla embarked on a mercy mission to return a freed prisoner to his home. On their way back to their mission, their jeep got stuck in a flood. Carla drowned and Ita survived. Ita remembers the accident: "Just then, the jeep turned over and the driver's side went down, the door closed and the river started to come in." At that moment, Carla pushed Ita through the window. "I went bobbing down the river and I couldn't believe it was so far down, I went down very deep and I said to myself, 'You're not going to get up,' so I said, 'Receive me, Lord.'" Several kilometers down stream, however, after a long time of turning, twisting, and being thrown against the river bottom, Ita was finally able to hold on to some roots. She recalled: "In a voice other them my own I said, 'The Lord has saved you to continue serving the poor and you've got to get out of this river.'"[15]

Several weeks after Carla's death, Jean left for a six-week vacation. She visited her parents, met her friend, Doug, and attended a friend's wedding in Ireland. Throughout this period, Doug, Father Crowley, and others tried to persuade Jean not to return to El Salvador. When she visited the Maryknoll Center in Ossining, her friends and colleagues there offered the same advice: Don't return. Yet Jean insisted that she had to return to El Salvador, because she had promised the children that she would come back to them.

Before leaving, Jean prayed for several hours in the Maryknoll chapel, emerging with a renewed sense of tranquillity. Before returning to El Salvador, Jean vacationed with her parents in Florida. "God straightened the whole thing out for me," she shared with her parents. She hoped that God would protect her from being tortured, but she was willing to give her life.

Her mother described her daughter during their visit: "She was the old Jeannie—happy." When Jean returned to El Salvador, she was peaceful and enthusiastic about her mission work.[16]

In the weeks before her death, Jean and the others busied themselves with providing transportation and supplies for the refugee center at Chalatenango. Although they knew they were in danger and that there had been death threats, they believed that being U.S. citizens would protect them from danger. On the afternoon of December 2,

Jean and Dorothy drove to the airport to pick up their colleagues, Maura Clarke and Ita Ford, who were returning from a conference in Nicaragua. By the time the four women left the airport, it was already dark for the five-mile drive home. They did not make it home—and were never heard from again. On December 4, their bodies were discovered in a shallow ditch.[17]

Jean's friend and confidant, Father Crowley, reflected on the meaning of Jean Donovan's life in an article published in *U.S Catholic:* "Underneath her happy, casual, nonchalant personality was a serious, committed person with a deep religious conviction, which explained her madness. I mean, by any standards of the 20th century, going down to Salvador and risking your life is a form of madness. But she knew what she was doing, and it fitted totally into her life's meaning, which was a commitment, I think to her Christianity."[18]

The profound courage of Jean Donovan, Ita Ford, Maura Clarke, and Dorothy Kazel—murdered on a deserted road in El Salvador—reminds us that "No one has greater love than this, to lay down one's life for one's friends" (John 15:13). These women faced fear with trust, overcame doubt with faith, and transformed hate with love. They lived the simplicity of the gospel in the midst of poverty, hunger, homelessness, civil war, torture, and death squads. These women loved the Salvadoran people with all their hearts. They worked tirelessly for justice in solidarity with the poor, took risks to serve homeless refugees, and shared the same fate as the poor in life and in death.

Jean's witness proclaims the powerful impact of single women who are heroes in our world today. Some of us, like Jean, will be called to give our lives as martyrs for the gospel. But God does not call most of us to so great a sacrifice. However, all of us are called to discern God's will for our lives. This involves listening, loving, and serving God, who speaks to us through the ordinary and extraordinary events of life—including birth, death, relationships, promotions, loses, sicknesses, successes, and failures. This implies stretching ourselves to the limits and discovering the greatness within ourselves.

Each person has a mission, a task, that no one else can do. This mission is our unique call to serve God and others in this world. As we respond to God's call we will encounter obstacles and challenges along the way, just as Jean did in her service to the poor and oppressed refugees in El Salvador. Yet nothing stopped her from keeping on with her mission. So, too, nothing will stop us from keeping on with our mission—no matter where it is, what it is, or for whom it is. Opposition, threats, condemnation, abuse, or violence by others will not hold us back. Our faithful God will walk with us and love us as we serve others, confront evil, and celebrate goodness, one step at a time and one day at a time. If we do this, we, like Jean, will be faithful to the end.

Reflection

At times I'm sure both my parents wonder where I got the mission calling. To me it's obvious after having two people such as my parents to grow with. My father is a gentle man. He has never been afraid to show love. I think I admire this about him best.... My mother is a very get-up-and-go person who always seems to have the energy to do something for someone else.[19]

Often there is a lot of frustration and pain involved as one cannot do enough, or anything at times. At times, one wonders if one should remain in such a crazy incredible mess. I only know that I am trying to follow where the Lord leads and, in spite of fear and uncertainty at times, I feel at peace and hopeful.[20]

Where else would you find roses in December?[21]

Discussion Starters

1. Jean Donovan was a successful career women who left it all behind to join the mission team in El Salvador. If you could interview Jean, what questions would you like to ask her?

2. Jean and her associates—Dorothy Kazel, Maura Clark, and Ita Ford—worked in solidarity with the oppressed people of El Salvador. What impact do you think their ministry had on the people they helped? What impact do you think the sufferings and death of the poor had on these Church women?

3. How did the murders of these women affect U.S. policy toward El Salvador? How can we join with others to change policies that support oppressive governments that violate human rights? What responsibility do we have as Christians to get involved in public policy debates that affect justice issues in our own country and around the world?

4. Jean Donovan was a woman of courage with a strong commitment to serve the poor people of El Salvador. What is your mission, your call, to serve God and others in this world? As you respond to God's call, what obstacles and challenges do you encounter along the way?

Prayer Experience

1. Close your eyes... Let your whole body relax... Imagine that you are at the top of ten steps... Take the first step down... Feel your muscles relax and become heavier as you slowly descend each step, all the way to the bottom...

2. Imagine that you are about to embark on a special journey to a place where you feel at peace, safe, and at home... It can be the ocean, the mountains, a river, a meadow, or a place you remember from childhood... Be conscious of the sights, smells, sounds, and special beauty that you discover there... Spend as much time as you like in this special place... Be aware that the Love of All Ages is with you...

3. Begin to walk forward from this special place... In the distance, see a house... As you approach the house, see a woman open the door... She introduces herself to you... Her name is Jean Donovan... Right away you feel at home in her presence... You walk with her through the house to a beautiful room... You sit down together for a chat... You ask questions... Listen to her story... Listen as she tells you something amazing...something challenging...something inspiring...something comforting...

4. Share your story with Jean... Tell her something you have not told anyone else... Share with her your mission, your call, to serve God and others in this world... Share with her an important goal you have ...a task you want to accomplish...a secret fear...a hidden hope...an unspoken dream...a new challenge... See Jean look into your eyes and listen with deep understanding... Realize that Jean is a kindred spirit...a wonderful companion...a special friend...

5. Imagine that Jean and you are now joined by an invisible band of "saints" composed of the oppressed people who have been martyred in El Salvador and other countries throughout the world during the last twenty years... Imagine that these saints are interceding for the poor, abandoned, abused, hungry, homeless, people of the world... Both of you join their joyous prayers, their songs, and their dances for liberation...for equality...for human dignity...for justice...for love... As you do so, you experience a new understanding of the power of the communion of the saints in solidarity with the poor...

6. Now you and Jean become aware that you are alone in the presence of the Love of All Ages... Rise together... Hold each other's hands for a few minutes... Now walk back through the house to the door... You and Jean hug each other... You leave Jean standing at the door as you walk farther and farther away...

7. As you return home, you carry Jean within your heart in the Love of All Ages... You feel Jean's courage uplift you... You feel Jean's hope inspire you... You feel Jean's love energize you... You offer thanks for your new friend...

Dancing with the Vision

20.

Thea Bowman

A Shooting Star

Bertha Bowman, who changed her name to Sister Thea when she became a nun, was born a Protestant in Canton, Mississippi, in 1937. Her parents were Mary Esther Coleman, a teacher, and Theon Edward Bowman, a doctor. She was the granddaughter of a slave. Because she was the daughter of older parents, Thea spent a great deal of time in the company of her parents and their circle of friends, many of whom were already grandparents and great-grandparents. These elders took it upon themselves to shape Thea's vision of life. She remembered her growing up years: "From their music, stories, faith traditions and love, I learned religious, cultural and survival values. I was taught to do my best, try my hardest and keep striving up the ladder. But at each rung I was to reach back and help a brother, sister or stranger receive the gift and pass it on and thus help create a more caring, sharing world."[1]

After discovering that her daughter could not read after five years in a public school, Thea's mother transferred her to Holy Child Jesus Catholic School, run by the Franciscan Sisters of Perpetual Adoration. Thea recalled that she and her friends enjoyed school, did well, and were taught to tutor those who needed help with their schoolwork. From this, Thea gained a sense of cooperation and responsibility for others. At the age of twelve, she surprised her parents with the news that she was going to become a Catholic.

In 1953, at the age of sixteen and a junior in high school, Thea decided to become a nun. "I had witnessed so many Catholic priests, brothers and sisters who had made a difference that was far reaching, I wanted to be part of the effort to help feed the hungry, find shelter for the homeless, and teach the children."[2]

In that same year Thea entered the Franciscan Sisters' community in La Crosse, Wisconsin. After professing first vows, Sister Thea began teaching at Blessed Sacrament School in La Crosse. Then in 1961, she moved back to Canton, Mississippi, and taught English and music at Holy Child Jesus Catholic High School.

After ten years of teaching secondary school, Thea started graduate studies in English at the Catholic University of America. Barbara Moran, who studied with Thea and was her dorm-mate, remembers the happy times. While she tried to curl and tease her hair up, Barbara shares, Thea tried to straighten and plait her hair—all this before the natural look became popular. Barbara also remembers the many late nights when the two of them studied for exams and completed research papers. Together, they shared their wisdom and life experiences. "'Don't try to trade on your color,' I warned Thea when she piled up used clothing intended for the poor all over our lounge and kitchenette. 'Black folks won't bite,' she insisted when I told her it was hard for me to relate to black students who came to our Christian Weekends for College Students."[3]

In 1972, after completing her doctorate, Thea traveled to Europe and studied during the summer at Oxford. Upon her return she accepted a teaching position at Viterbo College in La Crosse, and later chaired the English department and directed the Hallelujah Singers. The degrees helped open up opportunities for Thea to share her Black culture and spirituality.

When her parents became ill in 1978, Thea returned to Canton to care for them. At that time, she became a consultant and later the director of the Office of Intercultural Awareness for the Diocese of Jackson, Mississippi. She also became a teacher at Xavier University in New Orleans, about two hundred miles from Canton. She taught Black theology and the arts that foster Black expression in preaching, liturgy, and teaching within the Church. She spoke and sang at youth rallies, workshops, and services throughout the United States, Canada, and Africa.

In 1984 Thea was diagnosed with breast cancer that had metastasized to the lymph nodes and bones. That same year, both of Thea's parents died. When asked how she found the strength to carry on, Thea credited her early upbringing for helping her to preserver: "Old people in the black community taught us that we should serve the Lord until we die. We can even serve the Lord on our deathbeds or in any circumstances in life. If we have faith, hope and love we can pass it on."[4]

In 1985 Thea attended the Forty-third International Eucharistic Congress in Nairobi, Kenya. She also visited Zimbabwe and Nigeria. During that year the National Black Sisters' Conference recognized Thea with the Harriet Tubman Award and Viterbo College honored her with the Pope John XXIII Award.

The television program "60 Minutes" profiled Thea in 1987. CBS correspondent Mike Wallace, who interviewed Thea, was impressed by her joy, warmth, and determination to change the Church. He gave the following introduction on the TV program: "Today, at forty-nine, Sister Thea is still shaking people up, preaching in her African robes, not the traditional white Catholic litany but a new black Catholic Gospel powered by the conviction that when something is wrong, you change it."[5]

Traveling to Africa in 1988, Thea conducted workshops on racism for the Maryknoll sisters in Arusha, Tanzania. Regis College in Boston presented Thea with a honorary doctorate in that same year. Subsequently she received honorary doctorates from Xavier University, Clarke College, Sacred Heart University, College of Our Lady of the Elms, Boston College, Georgetown University, Saint Michael's College, Marygrove College, Viterbo College, and Spring Hill College.

In 1989 Thea spoke at the annual meeting of the American bishops at Seton Hall University. In the same year she received the U.S.

Catholic Award for promoting the cause of women and the Bishop Carroll T. Dozier Award from Christian Brothers College for fostering peace and justice. Also that year, Saint Michael's College incorporated the Sister Thea Bowman Black Catholic Education Foundation to promote Black Catholic education.

In April 1989, one year before she died, Thea went to Mercy College of Detroit to be the presenter for their second Women's Spirituality Conference. By that time, Thea was so sick that the organizers of the conference doubted that she would have the strength for her appearance. To everyone's amazement, however, at the appointed hour on the appointed day, Thea and the Detroit Archdiocesan Gospel Choir were in place center stage. Over her shoulders, she wore a beautiful stole embroidered with the names of women from the Hebrew Scriptures—in stark contrast to her bald, uncovered head, ravaged by the effects of chemotherapy. Brigid Johnson describes the powerful moment: "Thea was radiant! She had at times an impish smile as she invited us 'white folk' present to loosen up and put ourselves into the music. She spoke of Church, God, Jesus, people, relationship, respect, culture.... About 45 minutes into her performance, I was struck with the powerful realization that Thea Bowman was being priest to God's people. That whole group of several hundred of us was being lifted up in prayer. We were bonded as one body as Thea sat before us, her hand raised in blessing."[6]

"When I reflect on Thea Bowman, her life and work," reminisces Marie Augusta Neal, "the first thought I have is that she made the bishops dance. For some of them, it was a reluctant participation and some may have felt even a little discomfort but they danced and sang 'We shall overcome someday.'"[7] This ode points out to all that Thea's ministry in the 1980s was but the ongoing effort of the civil rights movement of the 1950s and 1960s. Thea's vision was to be a joyful prophet of a new multi-ethnic Church and world—a community of people without walls. By her association with the bishops, Thea demonstrated that one can choose to work to change the structures from within.[8]

Thea Bowman died on March 30, 1990, in Canton, Mississippi, and people from all over the world came to pay their respects and tribute to this courageous woman. Joseph A. Brown writes: "People gathered to celebrate the death and life of a prophet.... Like the prophets of Israel, she used her life, her thought and her activities as the medium and the message. Sister Thea did more than announce what she had seen and heard while on the long journey of her faith. She took on, became possessed by, the voice of the beloved community called the 'old folks,' the 'elders,' the 'ancestors' in the African-American theological tradition embodied by Sister Thea. The Songs of Faith created by these old folks became the reference and commentary for each and every prophetic performance of Sister Thea. 'Give me that old-time religion' was the beginning, and 'Done made my vow to the Lord' was the ending of the quintessential 'Thea Experience.'"[9]

Determined to have people understand and appreciate the religious experience of African-Americans, Thea often said: "Black American spirituality...is at once a response to and reflection on Black life and culture.... It is shaped by our self-description as Black, Negro, Creole or colored. Regardless of the circumstance, wherever Blacks have sought to find meaning, purpose, identity, community, worth, and God together, Black Spirituality has grown and flourished."[10]

As a creative educator, artistic dancer, powerful singer, and dynamic lecturer, Sister Thea left a tremendous legacy of gospel living that will inspire, instruct, and enlighten generations to come. In her native African dress, she made people clap their hands, dance, and sing. She promoted intercultural awareness, understanding, and pride in Black culture. Even TV correspondent Mike Wallace and the Roman Catholic bishops experienced the joy she exuded.

When Father John Ford asked her what he should say at her funeral, Thea instructed him: "Just say what Sojourner Truth said about her own eventual dying. Tell them what Sojourner Truth said: I'm not going to die. I'm going home like a shooting star."[11]

Reflection

In her address to the United States bishops assembled at Seton Hall University on June 17, 1989, Thea Bowman asked for empowerment for her people…. She began by singing "Sometimes I feel like a motherless child/ A long way from home," and she asked, "Can you hear me church, will you help me church? I'm a pilgrim in the journey looking for home, and Jesus told me the church is my home, and Jesus told me that heaven is my home and I have here no lasting city. Cardinals, archbishops, bishops: My brothers or church, please help me to get home."[12]

What does it mean to be black and Catholic? It means that I come to my church fully functioning. This doesn't frighten you, does it? I bring myself, my black self, all that I am, all that I have, all that I hope to become, I bring my whole history, my traditions, my experience, my culture, my African-American song and dance and gesture and movement and teaching and preaching and healing and responsibility as gift to the church.[13]

I bring a…spirituality [that] is contemplative and biblical and holistic, bringing to religion a totality of minds and imagination, of memory, of feeling and passion and emotion and intensity, of faith that is embodied, incarnate praise…a spirituality that is communal, that tries to walk and talk and work and pray and play together—even with the bishops.[14]

Now, bishops, I'm going to ask you all to do something. Cross your right hand over your left hand. You've got to move together to do that. All right now, walk with me. See, in the old days, you had to tighten up so that when the bullets would come, so that when the tear gas would come, so that when the dogs would come, so that when the horses would come, so that when the tanks would come, brothers and sisters would not be separated from one another.[15]

And you remember what they did with the clergy and the bishops in those old days, where they'd put them? Right up in front, to lead the people in solidarity with our brothers and sisters in the church who suffer in South Africa, who suffer in Poland, who suffer in Ireland, who suffer in Nicaragua, in Guatemala, in Northern Ireland, all over this world. We shall live in love.

> "We shall live in love
> We shall live in love
> We shall live in love today
> Deep in my heart,
> Deep in my heart I know I do believe,
> We shall live in love."
> That's all we've got to do: love the Lord
> to love our neighbor. Amen. Amen. Amen.
> Amen.[16]

Discussion Starters

1. As a teacher, singer, dancer, and lecturer, Sister Thea Bowman spread the gospel and promoted pride in Black culture. What are some of the qualities and values that Thea handed on to us?

2. Why was Thea's message to the U.S. bishops an important one?

3. What gifts do Black Catholics bring to Catholicism?

4. Enthusiastic about the religious experience of African-Americans, Thea often spoke and wrote about their spirituality. How is Black American spirituality a reflection of Black life and culture? How does Black music express the essence of Black spirituality?

Prayer Experience

(Use gospel music, soul music, jazz, blues, or the simple rhythm of a drum beat as background for this prayer reflection. Perhaps you could use music by Sister Thea.)

1. Begin by singing, humming, swaying, dancing, moving, to the music or beat... As you do so, open yourself to the energy of the Spirit breathing, living, moving, singing, dancing in you...

2. Black music reveals God as Creator, Liberator, Protector, Source of Strength. Black music affirms God is. Sister Thea tells us that God is mother and father, sister and brother, rock, shield, and sword. God is water when we're thirsty, food when we're hungry, our doctor, our lawyer, our everything, our life. As you continue to listen to the music, invite God to reveal to you who God is in your life now... Open yourself to the ways God is loving you...healing you...liberating you...empowering you... Be aware of any new images of God that emerge...

3. Reflect on ways you see the face of God incarnated in people today of different races...different cultures...different ethnic backgrounds... Invite God to reveal to you who God is in your sisters and brothers...

4. Be aware of any thoughts, feelings, insights, images, and sensations that occur as you do so... Record these in a journal or express them in some creative way, such as painting, drawing, sculpting, stamping, poetry, song, dance, mime, or movement.

5. Dialogue with Thea about any insights that occur to you as you reflect on her life and writings about Black spirituality or Black music...

6. Reflect on ways you can live in deeper solidarity with Black people in their journey to liberation from discrimination and oppression in the U.S. and in countries throughout the world... Imagine yourself joining with others to witness to human dignity, freedom, justice, and equality... Imagine, as Thea did, a community without walls... Sing, dance, move, sway, tap, or jump up and down in "body prayer" as you listen to the music and see this dream becoming a reality in our world.

7. As you continue to experience the Spirit moving through you in the music, reflect on ways that you can do something practical to bring about greater understanding, dialogue, and sharing with Blacks and other minorities in your community. Perhaps you can attend multi-cultural awareness programs in your area or study Black culture. Join a racially mixed faith, study, or political-action group to work on social concerns. Join a lobby group that works for affirmative action programs. Conclude your prayer experience by celebrating with, dancing with, moving with Sister Thea. Allow her joyful spirit and warm love to embrace you in the sounds of the music... Let her spirit speak to your heart... "We shall overcome... Deep in my heart I know... I do believe we shall overcome someday..." Amen.

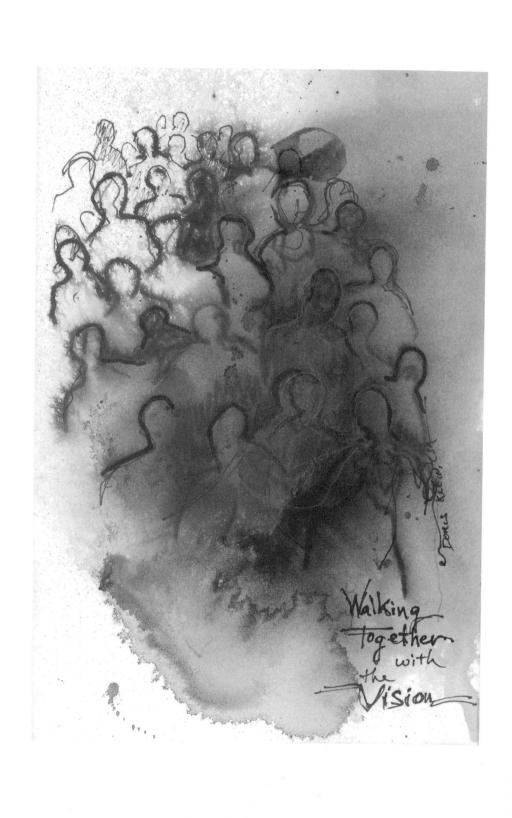

Doris Klein, CSA

Walking
together
with
the
Vision

Endnotes

1. Brigit of Kildare

1. Iain Macdonald. *Saint Bride*. Edinburgh: Floris Books, 1992.

2. Edward Sellner. *Wisdom of the Celtic Saints*. Notre Dame, Indiana: Ave Maria Press, 1993.

3. Macdonald, op. cit.

4. Ibid.

5. Ibid.

6. "Life of Brigit," cited in Sellner, op. cit.

7. Ibid.

8. Mary Condren. *The Serpent and the Goddess*. San Francisco: Harper and Row Publishers, 1989.

9. Macdonald, op. cit.

10. Thomas Cahill. *How the Irish Saved Civilization*. New York: Doubleday, 1995.

2. Margaret of Scotland

1. David Hugh Farmer. *Oxford Dictionary of Saints*. Oxford: Oxford University Press, 1992.

2. Ibid.

3. Joan Turpin. *Women in Church History*. Cincinnati: St. Anthony Messenger Press, 1990.

4. Ibid.

5. Ibid.

6. Ibid.

7. Farmer, op. cit.

8. Turpin, op. cit.

3. Hildegard of Bingen

1. Hildegard of Bingen, Prologue to *Scivias,* translated by Sabina Flanagan, *Secrets of God.* Boston: Shambhala Publishing, 1996.

2. *The Letters of Hildegard of Bingen,* vol. 1, translated by Joseph L. Baird and Radd K. Ehrman. New York: Oxford Press, 1994.

3. *Hildegard's Letters and the Acta,* translated by Sabina Flanagan, *Hildegard of Bingen: A Visionary Life.* New York: Routledge, Chapman, and Hall, 1989.

4. Matthew Fox. *Illuminations.* Sante Fe: Bear and Company, 1985.

5. Bernhard W. Scholz. "Hildegard von Bingen on the Nature of Women." *The American Review,* December 1980.

6. Fox, op. cit.

7. Gabrriele Uhlein. *Meditations With Hildegard of Bingen.* Sante Fe: Bear and Company, 1982.

8. Fox, op. cit.

9. Barbara Newman. *Sister of Wisdom.* Berkely: University of California Press, 1987.

4. Clare of Assisi

1. Ingrid J. Peterson. *Clare of Assisi: A Biographical Study.* Quincy, Illinois; Franciscan Press, 1993.

2. Carol Lee Flinders. *Enduring Grace.* San Francisco: HarperCollins, 1993.

3. Peterson, op. cit.

4. Flinders, op. cit.

5. *Peace Weavers*, edited by John Nichols and Lilian Thomas Shank. Kalamazoo, Michigan: Cistercian Publications, 1987.

6. Peterson, op. cit.

5. Julian of Norwich

1. *The Revelations of Divine Love,* edited by C. Wolters. New York: Penguin, 1966.

2. Ibid.

3. *Classics of Western Spirituality* Series. New York: Paulist Press, 1978.

4. Ibid.

5. Ibid.

6. Ibid.

6. Catherine of Siena

1. Carol Lee Flinders. *Enduring Grace*. San Francisco: HarperCollins, 1993.

2. Ibid.

3. Catherine of Siena. *The Dialogue,* translated by Suzanne Noffke. New York: Paulist Press, 1980.

4. Suzanne Noffke. *Catherine of Siena*. Collegeville, Minnesota: Liturgical Press, 1996.

5. Suzanne Noffke. *The Letters of Catherine of Siena*. Binghampton, New York: Center for Medieval and Early Renaissance Studies, 1988.

6. Ibid.

7. Joan of Arc

1. Louis de Conte. *Personal Recollections of Joan of Arc,* translated by Jean Francois Alden. New York and London: Harper and Brothers Publishers, 1906.

2. Anne Llewellyn Barstow. *Joan of Arc: Heretic, Mystic, and Shaman.* New York: Edwin Mellen Press, 1986.

3. Ibid.

4. W. S. Scott. *Jeanne d'Arc.* London: Harrap and Company, 1974.

5. Barstow, op. cit.

6. Ibid.

7. *Jeanne d'Arc, Maid of Orleans: As Set Forth in the Original Documents,* translated by T. Douglas Murray. New York: McClure, Phillips and Company, 1902.

8. Teresa of Avila

1. Francis Gross Jr. with Toni Perion Gross. *The Making of a Mystic.* Albany: State University of New York Press, 1993.

2. Victoria Lincoln. *Teresa: A Woman.* Albany: State University of New York Press, 1984.

3. Ibid.

4. Ibid.

5. Ibid.

6. Carol Lee Flinders. *Enduring Grace.* San Francisco: HarperCollins, 1993.

7. Ibid.

8. Sr. Mary, O.C.D. *Daily Readings With St. Teresa of Avila.* Springfield, Illinois: Templegate Publishers, 1985.

9. Carole Slade. *St. Teresa of Avila*. Berkely: University of California Press, 1995.

10. Joan Chittister. *A Passion for Life*. Maryknoll, New York: Orbis Books, 1996.

11. *The Bookmark Prayer of Teresa of Avila*

9. Louise de Marillac

1. Joan Turpin. *Women in Church History*. Cincinnati: St. Anthony Messenger Press, 1990.

2. *Butler's Lives of the Saints,* vol. 5. London: Virtue and Company Limited, 1961.

3. John F. Fenlon (Sermon on "The Works of Charity of Saint Louise of Marillac"). *Solemn Triduum in Honor of the Canonization of Saint Louise de Marillac*. (St. Joseph's) Emmitsburg, Maryland, 1934.

4. Butler, op. cit.

5. Turpin, op. cit.

6. Ibid.

7. Ibid.

8. Ibid.

9. Butler, op. cit.

10. Ibid.

11. Fenlon, op. cit.

10. Sor Juana Ines de la Cruz

1. Elizabeth Coonrod Martinez. *Sor Juana: A Trailblazing Thinker*. Brookfield, Connecticut: The Millbrook Press, 1994.

2. Ibid.

3. Octavio Paz. *Sor Juana*. Cambridge, Massachusetts; Harvard University Press, 1988.

4. Martinez, op. cit.

5. Paz, op. cit.

6. Ibid.

7. Ibid.

8. Ibid.

9. Martinez, op. cit.

10. Ibid.

11. Asuncion Lavrin. "Women and Religion in Spanish America" in *Women and Religion in America,* vol. 2, edited by Rosemary Radford Ruether and Rosemary Skinner Keller. San Francisco: Harper and Row Publishers, 1983.

12. *Sor Juana Ines de la Cruz,* edited by Frank de Varona. Milwaukee: Raintree Publishers, 1990.

13. Paz, op. cit.

14. Ibid.

15. Ibid.

16. Pope John Paul II. "Letter to Women" in *Origins*, July 27, 1995 vol 25, No. 9.

17. Teresa Malcolm. "Massachusetts women's group banned from church buildings in Boston." *National Catholic Reporter*, May 14, 1999.

18. Lavrin, op. cit.

11. Kateri Tekakwitha

1. Ellen H. Walworth. *The Life and Times of Kateri Tekakwitha:*

The Lily of the Mohawks. Buffalo, New York: Peter Paul and Bro., 1890.

2. *Women and Religion in America,* edited by Rosemary Radford Ruether and Rosemary Skinner Keller. San Francisco: Harper and Row Publishers, 1983.

3. Walworth, op. cit.

4. Ibid.

5. Justin C. Steurer. *The Impact of Katharine Tekakwitha on American Spiritual Life*. Washington, D.C.: The Catholic University of America, 1957.

6. Pierre Cholenec, S.J. *La Vie de Catherine Tegaskouita, premiere vierge Iroquise*. New York: Fordham University Press, 1940.

7. Steurer, op. cit.

8. Walworth, op. cit.

9. Ibid.

10. Steurer, op cit.

11. Ibid.

12. Walworth, op. cit.

13. Walworth, op. cit.

12. Elizabeth Bayley Seton

1. Annabelle M. Melville. *Elizabeth Bayley Seton*. New York: Charles Scribner's Sons, 1951.

2. Ibid.

3. Ibid.

4. Margaret Alderman and Josephine Burns. *Praying With Elizabeth Seton*. Winona, Minnesota: St. Mary's Press, 1992.

5. *Elizabeth Seton: Selected Writings*, edited by Ellin Kelly and

Annabelle Melville. New York: Paulist Press, 1987.

6. Melville, op. cit.

7. Alderman and Burns, op. cit.

8. Melville, op. cit.

9. Kelly and Melville, op. cit.

10. Alderman and Burns, op. cit.

13. Elizabeth Lange

1. According to the Oblate Archives, Joubert Diary, individual manuscripts, and oral tradition, Elizabeth Lange was born around 1784, in San Domingo, now Haiti. She left Cuba for Baltimore, then a haven for refugees from Hispaniola, the island which is made up of modern-day Dominican Republic and Haiti. This information is found in Maria M. Lannon, *Response to Love, The Story of Mother Mary Elizabeth Lange, O.S.P.,* Washington, D.C.: Josephite Pastoral Center, 1992.

2. Lannon, op. cit.

3. Ibid.

4. Ibid.

5. Ibid.

6. Joan Turpin. *Women in Church History*. Cincinnati: St. Anthony Messenger Press, 1990.

7. Lannon, op. cit.

8. Ibid.

9. Turpin, op. cit.

10. Lannon, op.cit.

11. Turpin, op cit.

12. Lannon, op. cit.

13. Turpin, op. cit.

14. Lannon, op. cit.

15. Ibid.

16. Ibid.

17. Ibid.

18. Turpin, op. cit.

19. Ibid.

20. Ibid.

21. Lannon, op. cit.

22. Ibid.

23. Ibid.

24. Ibid.

14. Sojourner Truth

1. Carleton Mabee. *Sojourner Truth: Slave, Prophet, Legend.* New York: New York University Press, 1993.

2. Ibid.

3. *Narrative of Sojourner Truth*, edited by Margaret Washington. New York: Vintage Books, 1993.

4. Ibid.

5. Mabee, op. cit.

6. Washington, op. cit.

7 Ibid.

8. Mabee, op. cit.

9. Ibid.

10. Washington, op. cit.

11. Norman L. Macht. *Sojourner Truth*. New York: Chelsea House Publishers, 1992.

12. Ibid.

13. Patricia C. McKissack and Frederick McKissack. *Sojourner Truth: Ain't I a Woman?* New York: Scholastic Inc., 1992.

14. Mabee, op. cit.

15. Ibid.

16. Jeri Ferris. *Walking the Road to Freedom*. Minneapolis: Carolrhoda Books, Inc., 1988.

17. Ibid.

18. McKissack and McKissack, op. cit.

15. Frances Xavier Cabrini

1. Theodore Maynard. *Too Small A World: The Life of Francesca Cabrini*. Milwaukee: The Bruce Publishing Company, 1945.

2. Reverend Abbot Smith, C.R.L., D.D. *Frances Xavier Cabrini: The Saint of the Emigrants*. London: The Catholic Book Club.

3. Maynard, op. cit.

4. Ibid.

5. Ibid.

6. Anne Fremantle. *Saints Alive*. Garden City, New York: Doubleday and Company, Inc., 1978.

7. Pietro Di Donato. *Immigrant Saint: The Life of Mother Cabrini*. New York: McGraw-Hill Book Company, 1960.

8. Ibid.

9. Ibid.

10. Fremantle, op. cit.

11. A.M. Melville. "St. Frances Xavier Cabrini." *New Catholic Encyclopedia*, Vol 2. Washington D.C.: The Catholic University of America, 1967.

12. Maynard, op. cit.

13. Fremantle, op. cit.

14. Di Donato, op. cit.

15. Ibid

16. Maynard, op. cit.

17. Di Donato, op. cit.

18. Maynard, op. cit.

16. Therese of Lisieux

1. *The Autobiography of St. Therese of Lisieux, The Story of a Soul,* translated by John Beevers, Garden City, New York: Doubleday and Company, 1957.

2. Ibid.

3. *Story of a Soul,* translated by John Clarke, O.C.D. ICS Publications, Washington Province of Discalced Carmelite Friars, 2131 Lincoln Rd. N.E., Washington, D.C. 20002, 1975, 1976.

4. Beevers, op. cit.

5. Ibid.

6. Ibid

7. Clarke, op. cit.

8. Ibid.

9. H. D. Kreilkamp, "'Little Flower': A Likely Doctor of Church for an Age of Anxiety," *National Catholic Reporter*, October 24, 1997.

10. *The Letters of St. Therese of Lisieux*. 2 volumes, translated by John Clarke, O.C.D. ICS Publications, Washington Province of Discalced Carmelite Friars, 2131 Lincoln Rd. N.E., Washington, D.C. 20002, 1982, 1988.

17. Dorothy Day

1. Dorothy Day. *Loaves and Fishes*. New York: Harper and Row Publishers, 1963.

2. Dorothy Day. *The Long Loneliness*. San Francisco: Harper and Row Publishers, 1952.

3. Mel Piehl. *Breaking Bread*. Philadelphia: Temple University Press, 1982.

4. Nancy L. Roberts. *Dorothy Day and the Catholic Worker*. Albany: Albany State University of New York Press, 1984.

5. Day. *The Long Loneliness*. op. cit.

6. Ibid.

7. Ibid.

8. Robert Coles. *Dorothy Day: A Radical Devotion*. Reading, Massachusetts: Addison-Wesley Publishing Company, 1987.

9. George M. Anderson. "Dorothy Day Centenary," *America*, November 29, 1997.

10. Dorothy Day. "A Room for Christ," *The Catholic Worker*, December 1945.

18. Catherine de Hueck Doherty

1. Catherine de Hueck Doherty. *Fragments of My Life*. Notre Dame, Indiana: Ave Maria Press, 1979.

2. Ibid.

3. Ibid.

4. Emile Briere. *Katia*. Sherbrooke, Quebec: Editions Paulines, 1988.

5. Doherty, op. cit.

6. Catherine de Hueck Doherty. *Poustinia*. Notre Dame, Indiana: Ave Maria Press, 1974.

7. Helen Cecilia Swift and Margaret N. Telscher. *Unveiling the Feminine Face of the Church*. Cincinnati: St. Anthony Messenger Press, 1989.

8. Doherty. *Fragments*, op. cit.

9. Swift and Telscher, op. cit.

10. Ibid.

11. Doherty. *Poustinia*, op. cit.

12 Briere, op. cit.

13. Doherty. *Poustinia,* op. cit.

14. Ibid.

15. For more information about Madonna House, contact Madonna House Apostolate, Combermere, Ontario, Canada KOJ ILO, 613–756–3713.

16. Catherine de Hueck Doherty. *Urodivoi: Fools For God*. New York: Crossroad, 1983.

17. Ibid.

19. Jean Donovan

1. Joe Lynch. "Jean Donovan's Legacy to her Parents: Footsteps of Faith." *Sojourners*, June 1987.

2. Ibid.

3. Ibid.

4. Ibid.

5. Ibid.

6. Judith M. Noone. *The Same Fate as the Poor*. New York: Maryknoll Sisters Publication, 1984.

7. Lynch, op. cit.

8. Ibid.

9. Joan Turpin. *Women in the Church*. Cincinnati: St. Anthony Messenger Press, 1990.

10. Ibid.

11. Ibid.

12. Helen Cecilia Swift and Margaret N. Telscher. *Unveiling the Feminine Face of the Church*. Cincinnati: St. Anthony Messenger Press, 1989.

13. Turpin, op. cit.

14. Ibid.

15. Noone, op. cit.

16. Turpin, op. cit.

17. Ibid.

18. Swift and Telscher, op. cit.

19. Turpin, op. cit.

20. Swift and Telscher, op. cit.

21. Turpin, op. cit.

20. Thea Bowman

1. "She Inspires Thousands But Who Inspires Her?" reprinted from *CUA Magazine*, Washington, D.C.: Catholic University, Winter 1990.

2. Ibid.

3. Christian Koontz. *Thea Bowman: Handing on her Legacy.* Kansas City: Sheed and Ward, 1991.

4. *CUA Magazine*, op. cit.

5. *Sister Thea Bowman: Shooting Star,* edited by Celestine Cepress. Winona, Minnesota: St. Mary's Press, 1993.

6. Koontz, op. cit.

7. Ibid.

8. Ibid.

9. Ibid.

10. "Spirituality: The Soul of the People," reprinted from *Tell It Like It Is: A Black Catholic Perspective on Christian Education.* Oakland, CA: National Black Sisters Conference [NBSC], 1983.

11. "A Shooting Star," reprinted from Trinity Missions (Winter 1990): 5, used with permission of Trinity Missions.

12. Cepress, op. cit.

13. Ibid.

14. Ibid.

15. Ibid.

16. Ibid.

Recommended Reading

Condren, Mary. *The Serpent and the Goddess*. San Francisco: Harper and Row Publishers, 1989.

A comprehensive work filled with fascinating material demonstrating the egalitarian vision of early Celtic life. This book is an important contribution in Celtic feminist literature. The images and stories of Brigit will appeal to generations of Celtic women and people who want to know more about the Celtic spirit.

Silent Voices, Sacred Lives: Women's Readings for the Liturgical Year, edited by Barbara Bowie, Kathleen Hughes, Sharon Karam, and Carolyn Osiek. New York: Paulist, 1992.

This groundbreaking book combines the Scriptures, intertestamental literature, noncanonical Christian sources, Church orders, mystical works, poetry, Gnostic writings, diaries, accounts of martyrdom, epitaphs, and descriptions for women at worship. Together these accounts enrich our repertoire in the ways God communicates with us and the ways women reflect and image God. This book deserves careful reading and deep reflection.

Byrne, Lavinia. *The Hidden Tradition: Women's Spiritual Writings Rediscovered*. New York: Crossroad, 1991.

This anthology is drawn from different Christian traditions, such as Hildegard of Bingen to twentieth-century writers such as Dorothy Sayers, Edith Stein, and Evelyn Underhill. It reveals the extraordinary depth and power of women's relationship with the Holy One, and will enable readers to reflect on the rich treasury of women's writings through the centuries. This book provides a wonderful resource to discover women's writings that, for a long time, were hidden but are now emerging from their shadowy, nameless place in the Christian tradition.

Chittister Joan. *A Passion for Life*. Maryknoll, New York: Orbis Books, 1996.

A beautifully illustrated book, with color icons by Robert Lentz, guaranteed to stir your soul. Sister Joan tells the story of some of the most prominent activists, mystics, and prophets of the ages, such as Hagar, Amos, Mary Magdalene, Mother Jones, Pedro Arrupe, Oscar Romero, Thomas Merton, Catherine of Siena, John XXIII, and many more. They are all "heroes," "stars," or "icons." Yet they are also people who are like ourselves in many ways. Reading this book is like listening to Joan preach, an experience that is both inspiring and challenging. A "must-read."

Fiorenza, Elizabeth Schussler. *In Memory of Her*. New York: Crossroad, 1983.

This scholarly treatise brings to consciousness women who played an important role in the origins of Christianity. It represents a shift from an androcentric to a feminist interpretation and reconstruction of women's early Christian history. It is groundbreaking and must reading for students of the early Church and New Testament, and for feminists. This book is a first within the discipline of New Testament studies.

Mabee, Carleton. *Sojourner Truth: Slave, Prophet, Legend*. New York: New York University Press, 1993.

Pulitzer prize-winning author Carleton Mabee vividly brings to life one of the great champions of Black emancipation and women's rights. I read it as a good, popular history about a Black woman striving for personal and political empowerment. I learned from her extensive scholarship, her choice of powerful scenes, and her careful selection of dialogue. This compelling analysis of the legendary Sojourner Truth sheds new light on the little-known world of Northern slavery and provides an inspiring account of the spiritual journey of the most enigmatic Black woman of the nineteenth century.

Meehan, Bridget Mary. *Praying With Women of the Bible*. Liguori: Liguori Publications, 1998.

The twenty women depicted—women from both Hebrew and Christian Scriputres—stand forth as prophets, visionaries, activists, saints, martyrs, and heroines. As radiant reflections of the feminine face of God, their lives epitomize women liberation, women courage, women strength, and women passion. Ideal for individual and group use, each entry begins with a brief biography and Scripture story, followed by discussion questions and prayer experiences. A wonderful resource for adolescent girls and women who are looking for women mentors in the Bible.

Nunnally-Cox, Janice. *ForeMothers*. New York: Seabury, 1981.

Janice Nunnally-Cox presents the women of the Hebrew and Christian Scriptures. In a clear and popular style, this book discusses the story of biblical women, such as Sara and Hagar, Leah and Rachel, Dinah, Miriam, Deborah and Jael, Hannah, Michal and Abigail, the woman with a hemorrhage, the Syrophoenician woman, the adulterous woman, Tabitha, Euodia, and Syntyche. This is a helpful resource for all persons interested in women in the Bible, and an inspiration for contemporary women and men in their search for God.

O'Connor, Francis Bernard. *Like Bread, Their Voices Rise*. Notre Dame, Indiana: Ave Maria, 1993.

In this thought-provoking book, Francis Bernard O'Connor demonstrates that Catholic women all over the world need to be included as equals—and such is not yet the case. Crossing cultural and institutional barriers, she examines key issues and raises important questions in the life of Catholic women in the United States, Brazil, Bangladesh, and Uganda. She challenges the Vatican's assumption that women's desire for full participation in the Church is only a North American issue, and reveals that there are striking similarities between the experiences and hopes of women from these four continents.

Women and Religion in America, edited by Rosemary Radford Ruether and Rosemary Skinner Keller. San Francisco: Harper and Row Publishers, 1981.

This is an excellent investigation of the impact and role of women in religion during the nineteenth century. The authors of this trail-blazing work, the first of three volumes, seek to recover the feminine experience in seven essays by seven women scholars—each documented by interesting letters, journal entries, and biographical excerpts of religious pioneer women from many cultural, social, and racial spheres. The women who appear on these pages are a notable group—deaconesses, laypeople, and nuns. They founded new religious movements and contributed efforts to laity rights, social and utopian reform movements, and women's ordination.

Sleevi, Mary Lou. *Sisters and Prophets.* Notre Dame, Indiana: Ave Maria Press, 1993.

Mary Lou Sleevi's sacred art and stories portray twelve women of faith. Through their visionary lives and prophetic voices, we learn new things about ourselves and God. Like her previous bestseller, *Women of the Word* (Ave Maria Press, 1989), this beautiful book invites us to contemplate the strength and courage of our spiritual foremothers.

Winter, Miriam Therese. *WomanWord.* New York: Crossroad, 1990.

This feminist lectionary provides creative celebrations that include biographical information, shared discussion questions, and original psalms on New Testament women, such as Anna, the woman who anoints Jesus' head, the poor widow, the woman at the well, Martha and Mary, Mary Magdalene, Jairus' daughter, Rhoda, Lydia, Phoebe, Prisca, Peter's mother-in-law, Lois, Eunice, and many others.

Winter, Miriam Therese. *WomanWisdom*. Part One. New York: Crossroad, 1991.

Liturgist Miriam Therese Winter presents fifty provocative celebrations for women of the Hebrew Scriptures—both women whose stories have been told (like Eve and Sarah and Rebekah) and women whose stories must be told (like Cozi and Zipporah and Keturah). *WomanWisdom* is a powerful book for women—and men—of all denominations who want to celebrate our foremothers and foresisters in the faith.

Winter, Miriam Therese. *WomanWitness*. Part Two. New York: Crossroad, 1992.

In this last of her three companion volumes, Miriam Therese Winter presents fifty more services for women of the Hebrew Scriptures. There are innovative liturgies for women, like Tamar, Poiphar's wife, Pharaoh's daughter, Deborah, Delilah, Ruth, Naomi, Bathsheba, Jezebel, and the women often forgotten: the prostitutes, midwives, maids, servants, and slaves.

Zimmer, Mary. *Sister Images*. Nashville: Abingdon Press, 1993.

This is a collection of twenty commentaries and guided imagery meditations written especially to help contemporary women make connections between their own lives and those of their female biblical sisters. It is ideal for personal devotion, spiritual formation, and study groups. This book bridges the gap between biblical interpretation, feminist theology, and women in the Church.

Sheed & Ward

Other Books of Interest

available at your favorite bookstore

Delighting in the Feminine Divine

Bridget Mary Meehan

Hebrew Scriptures, Jesus-Sophia, the witness of the early Church, and in contemporary society, this book will help you pray and uncover diverse and inclusive images of God. Art work and text blend to show the challenge and expanded spiritual sensibilities that can be found in these new ways to vision, live, and pray.

142 pp 1-55612-658-1 *$9.95*

Wisdom's Feast

Sophia in Study and Celebration

Susan Cole, Marian Ronan & Hal Taussig

Imaging and interacting with Sophia as the feminine face of God. Moving from ancient biblical references to present day context, the authors skillfully stage a series of participative liturgies.

240 pp 1-55612-856-8 *$14.95*

Psalms of a Laywoman

Edwina Gateley

New Gift Edition of a Modern Classic

Following the familiar and powerful style of the biblical Psalms, Gateley openly reflects on her life and ministry, and ultimately on the nature of faith itself. With a poet's eye and a believer's heart, Gateley reveals the metaphysical in the practical, the mystical in the ordinary, the divine in the human. Her psalms are a call to recognize God's presence in each of our lives.

142 pp 1-58051-052-3 *$9.95*

The Feminization of the Church?

Kaye Ashe, O.P.

Ashe explores the extent and nature of the feminization of the Church. How has it affected women and spirituality, language, ethics, ministry, and leadership? How is the Church reacting to this feminization, and how is it affecting the life and future of the Church itself?

168 pp 1-58051-028-0 *$14.95*

SHEED & WARD

An Apostolate of the Priests of the Sacred Heart

30 Amberwood Parkway
Ashland, OH 44805

Email www.bookmasters.com/sheed *Phone* 1-800-266-5564 or *Fax* 419-281-6883